INDIANS OF NEW MEXICO

EDITED BY RICHARD C. SANDOVAL
AND REE SHECK

DESIGNED AND PRODUCED BY
RICHARD C. SANDOVAL

EDNA S. GLENN
EDITORIAL CONSULTANT, PROFESSOR
COLLEGE OF SANTA FE

TYPESETTING BY LINDA J. VIGIL

PUBLISHED BY

NEW MEXICO MAGAZINE

Pottery making is traditionally considered a woman's craft, while men usually paint the designs on pieces. Blue Corn's son Craig now designs the patterns that adorn her pottery, such as the feather bowls above. Blue Corn says that although Craig, another son and a grandson have taken an interest in pottery making, it is her daughters who will inherit the tools of the craft passed on to her by her grandmother.

All designs have a meaning, says Blue Corn's son Craig, who learned the art by watching his older brother Joseph, who in turn studied the designing process with their late father, Santiago. Craig says the tradition is learned only by observation and no formal training is involved.

She says the tradition of giving Indian names was passed on by her mother, who chose another woman not related to the family to name her.

Blue Corn says she always makes an exact double of every one of her creations in case one is damaged in the firing process, one of the most difficult and crucial steps in pottery making.

Blue Corn, who travels throughout the country teaching workshops on her craft, says handmade bowls and plates played an important role in domestic life of the pueblo in the past. "Now we only make them for tourists," she says. Blue Corn is the name given to the potter by the late María Martínez's older sister. Blue Corn hasn't used her birth-given name since she started making pottery.

The Storytellers
Louis and Virginia Naranjo
craft stories in clay

by Charles B. Rosenak
Photography by Mark Nohl

As a child, I was blue-suited and led by mother's hand past two pieces of Cochití pottery dating from the 1870s. Housed in Chicago's Field Museum of Natural History, they stand sentinel to the mystic realm of the American Indian.

These two satirical figurines depicting Spanish dons were created by unknown hands from Cochití clay, but Louis and Virginia Naranjo of Cochití Pueblo, if they were ever to venture as far east as Chicago, would recognize with pride that, as Louis is fond of saying, "they were made in the old way, as they were supposed to be made."

Louis and Virginia Naranjo are currently standard-bearers for the proud figurative pottery tradition of Cochití pueblo, just west of Interstate 25, between Santa Fe and Albuquerque. "It's the way of our old people," Louis says in an almost chant, "and I want to keep it up."

Louis and Virginia were both born in 1932. They grew up together in the pueblo and were married in 1961. To date, the couple have three children and four grandchildren, all living in the village. Louis and Virginia love to babysit while they sculpt their figurines at the dining room table in their comfortable adobe house. They make pottery almost every non-feast day: "We don't keep hours, but I don't work at night—bad for the eyes," Louis says. The Naranjos craft their art slowly and with great care, joking and exchanging the gossip of the day as they go along, accompanied by television, children and grandchildren. It's a good life.

Figurative pottery is alive and well in Cochití today, despite the efforts of the Spanish to destroy it as the making of idols. In fact, there is evidence to suggest that this resilient tradition was merely in a state of decline just before Helen Cordero revived its popularity with a bang in 1964. The hunger of tourists to bring a little something home

spelled an almost instant success for Helen's storytellers.

"Helen was given the credit," Virginia will acknowledge, "but Louis' grandmother Frances Suina, living across the street from Helen, was doing it at the same time. She was making small animals and maidens with babies on their backs. She may have taught Helen."

Virginia was the first in the Naranjo family to make pottery. She was making small bowls under the watchful eye of a great aunt by the age of 10—by 1962 she was making small animals. Shortly after Louis and Virginia were married, they started exhibiting at Indian Market, an annual August event in Santa Fe that draws collectors, tourists and dealers from around the world to the colorful Plaza to view and purchase Native American wares. In the early years, Louis sold drums (Cochití is renowned for its drum makers) and Virginia offered beadwork.

Then, in 1976, Virginia brought a large clay turtle she had crafted to Indian Market and walked away with her first blue ribbon. The Naranjos had found their thing. From 1976 to 1989, they won at least one blue ribbon for figurative pottery at market each year.

It wasn't all easy sledding. In 1980, Virginia suffered a stroke, fell and broke her right arm. For four or five years Louis had to continue the work pretty much on his own. Virginia continued to help him on technical matters, but it was from Louis' fertile imagination that the great figurative pottery of this period flowed. It wasn't until 1987 or so that Virginia really began to sculpt again.

Louis instantly took to the clay: "It likes me, and I like it," he lovingly states. "If you don't like the clay and don't have good intentions, you can't even find it. You have to talk to it."

The clay comes from the hills of Cochití, the white slip

Tablita Dancers

Buffalo Dancers

from Santo Domingo Pueblo and the red from Bandelier. "Nothing is commercial," Louis explains. "The black is from beeweed, which grows near the village. We boil it down to juice. It goes on green and turns black when you fire. Nothing holds to the white slip like beeweed."

The pottery is fired in the old way, too: placed on a metal grill over a cedar fire, protected by wire and covered with cow chips. Virginia says that the "cow chips must be a dry gray or else the heat from the fire won't soak back into the clay." There is great uncertainty whenever the Naranjos fire. They are never sure that the finished product will meet their expectations. If the wind is wrong or something isn't dry enough, the figures will have smudges of gray in the white. This phenomenon is common and doesn't bother Cochití potters, but collectors prefer the whites to be creamy and pure.

Coyotes

Creche in the Lap of the Angel

Mother and Child

Black or Red?
Potter reveals secrets of her art

Since the days of María Martínez, art collectors have prized the polished black pottery of San Ildefonso and Santa Clara pueblos.

While this work is much appreciated, the process by which it is formed is often misunderstood. Books on Tewa Indian black pottery all agree that the final stage of firing is crucial. But the experts disagree on what's happening to cause the pots to turn black. Some say the coloring occurs because the fire is smothered with dried manure. Others maintain that the smothering creates a carbon smoke that penetrates the pottery, turning it black.

To clear up the mystery, we asked retired Los Alamos chemist Luke Lyon (now deceased) to conduct formal experiments and to interview his longtime friend Reycita Naranjo, a Santa Clara potter, on the secrets of how she creates her exquisite black pottery. A member of a prominent family of Santa Clara artisans, Naranjo is the daughter of Pablita Chavarria, who was featured in a 1963 film on pottery making produced by the American Indian Films Group. Naranjo herself has won prizes at the Indian Market in Santa Fe, the New Mexico State Fair and numerous arts and crafts shows sponsored by the Eight Northern Pueblos. She agreed to provide Lyon a step-by-step account of the way she works.

Lyon's specialty at the lab in Los Alamos was high-temperature carbon chemistry, but he also wrote more than 20 articles on ethnohistory. Working with Barton Olinger, another Los Alamos scientist, Lyon carried out experiments that disproved that carbon deposits have anything to do with black coloring in pots. Reporting on his findings, he wrote, "Even though several books describing black Pueblo pottery attribute the color to carbon, the reduction of iron oxide is the correct mechanism. Ceramicists, describing ancient styles of Old World pottery, state that iron impurities in clay form red oxide at red heat, but if air is lacking during firing, the iron impurities form black magnetite."

Following is Naranjo's narrative.

↓ ↓ ↓

"We get our clay at several places on the reservation, but I get mine in those hills up behind the health clinic. It is reddish brown and wet. We dry it, break it up into small lumps, sift it and take out any limestone or pebbles. We soak the dry lumps in water for a day and a half. We add volcanic sand to the clay. . . . If we don't put enough sand into the clay, then the pottery breaks in the firing. They just blow up. If we put too much in, it doesn't polish. It scratches."

Interview by Luke Lyon
Photography by Stephen Trimble

Reviewing the pot-firing process, Naranjo says, "I start from the bottom and put cow chips all around and go up and then cover the whole thing. It is best to fire on a day when the weather is calm—no wind, not raining or anything. The firing takes about two hours. After the fire is all smothered with horse manure, we brush away the manure and unburned cow chips. We take the tins (covering the pottery) off one by one, and two of us pick the tray of pottery up and take it out of the fire area."

↓ ↓ ↓

Reycita Naranjo, holding an 1890s Santa Clara pot from the Laboratory of Anthropology collection, discusses the black coloring of this distinctive work. "What I think makes the pots black is the red-clay paint that we polish with and the manure that we use in firing. That is how I figure it, because if you want red pots, you don't use manure and they come out red. If you use manure, they come out black."

Before firing a pot in a kiln such as this one, Naranjo must complete an elaborate series of preparations.

"If I form a pot today, I let it stand there tonight. Next morning I go over the pot again to shape it up. Then I let it stand there for one night and one day. I look at the piece and study it. I draw on it with a pencil. After I finish designing it, I carve it up with a paring knife and set it out to dry . . . little ones for about a week, big ones about two weeks. I like to be in a closed section of the house. If you open the door, the wind comes through, it hits the pot and uneven drying causes it to crack.

"After drying, we use sandpaper to get out rough parts, dents and gourd marks.

"Then we polish it. I buy the red clay I use for the paint from Santo Domingo. A lump of it just forms a red paint when put into water. I put the paint [a mixture of clay and iron oxide] on all the parts I want to polish. I polish with the stones handed down to me from my mother. Then I put a little bit of bacon grease all over and let it dry to a grayish color. Where I want the pot to come out dull, I take a brush and paint with the same red clay paint I used on the first polishing. And all the parts are now bright red from the clay paint and the polishing. I use gloves so I don't leave any marks or fingerprints."

"As a little girl, as my mother Pablita [Tafoya] Chavarria was making pottery, I would start little figurines. She would straighten them out and make them into something. That is how I learned. That is how she learned, but she had to push herself because her mother died when Pablita was 12 years old. This aunt of hers helped her. That is how I think everybody learned their pottery-making art.

"I learned shapes from her: wedding vase, basket, bowls, big vases, figurines, turtles. And I learned her designs, too: feather designs, squash blossom, clouds, bear claw, mountain figures, kiva steps and Avanyu, the Rain Serpent . . . all these I learned from her. She had seven daughters. There are really five of us sisters who are doing it now: Clara Shije, Elizabeth Naranjo, Florence Browning, Mary Singer and myself. Some of their children and my daughter-in-law Jennifer Naranjo are doing it. My two grandsons come home from school and when I'm doing pottery, they get in there and they are interested in it, too."

Talking With Clay

At Picurís Pueblo, cradled by green forest in New Mexico's Sangre de Cristo Mountains, when the Pueblo Indian village prepares to replaster its adobe church, the workers make a pile of dirt next to the old mission. From this soil gathered for mud plaster glint the sharp edges and faded designs of broken pieces of pottery; potsherds from generations past become a part of the church to be used by generations into the next century.

At Taos, the elders ask a young potter to make a bowl for ceremonial use in the kiva. Her first effort they reject; it looks too new. They want one blackened with smoke, and so she refires her bowl, smudging it black. The elders are satisfied.

Isleta Pueblo, southward along the Río Grande, celebrates its feast day every year on the fourth of September. After Mass, the people carry a carved image of St. Augustine in procession around the plaza. Near the shrine on the far side of the square, where the saint will be honored, a Pueblo woman offers food to the carved *santo.* She walks to the head of the procession with a pottery bowl of steaming chile stew and wafts the steam toward the saint's unmoving face, under the approving eyes of the village priest.

"We come into this world with pottery and we are going to leave the earth with pottery," says Ácoma Pueblo potter Dolores García. Ácomas are bathed in a pottery bowl at birth and buried with pottery when they melt back into the earth. Pottery is a tradition, but it is also a part of contemporary life. It is art—vital everyday art. Maxine Tafoya of Jémez says, "It is not just an art, it is a very spiritual art." And it is both a creation and a symbol of the Pueblo people.

Pueblo pottery comes from the earth. It is made with clay, painted with minerals and plants, shaped with stones and gourds. Pueblo artists take these pieces of the land and make pottery, and in doing so they create a bond between land and people. Blue Corn says of her fellow San Ildefonso potters: "Doing this pottery making in the traditional way—with their hands, without using a machine at all—it's really a miracle. To them and to me, too."

This miracle starts with what most of us call dirt: with clay. Pueblo potters often speak of "picking" clay, as they would pick flowers. Clay is a gift from Mother Earth, and like all of her gifts, it is sacred.

Digging clay is hard physical labor. Men often help their wives and daughters with this task, making it a family outing. Derek de la Cruz helps his wife, Santa Clara potter Lois Gutiérrez, gather clay. He says, "If you look hard enough, you can find clay here and there all over the mountains, but it doesn't just jump out at you." Stella Teller of Isleta says that it takes 65 percent of her time to gather and process the materials for potting—just preparing for the creative act.

🕊 🕊 🕊

Opposite—The melon bowls were made by Helen Shupla of Santa Clara Pueblo and are courtesy of Richard M. Howard.

Text and photography by Stephen Trimble

Not only do the potters dig, soak and clean the clay, but they must collect and prepare the temper they mix with it. Northern Río Grande Pueblo people temper their clay with ground volcanic ash and tuff. For six centuries, Zía potters have used finely ground basalt—laboriously hand grinding the hard rocks on a *mano* and *metate*. And at Ácoma, Laguna and Zuñi the artists manufacture their temper by grinding old pottery sherds to add to fresh clay. Modern Ácoma pottery may contain several succeeding generations of pots within its clay.

The men help in the hard work of mixing clay or in painting, and today, males make fine pottery. Virginia Gutiérrez at Pojoaque believes men make better potters than women: "They have more of an artistic ability." Jenny Laate, an Ácoma who teaches pottery making at Zuñi High School, says, "My boys turn out better than the girls. Girls get discouraged too fast." Ácoma potter Stella Shutiva says, "Men are strong. They make big pots, pots shaped the way their bodies are shaped, narrow at the base and wider at the top. Women make pots that are plumped."

Rose Naranjo, from Santa Clara, says, "The clay is very selfish. It will form itself to what the clay wants to be." The clay forms itself, but if the potter has "a good intention," is "one with the clay," the pot will please both the clay and the shaper. It will be an extension of the individual potter's spirit.

More than anything else, coiling defines Pueblo pottery: it is built by hand, never thrown on a wheel. Ernest Tapia at Santa Clara says, "If we use a wheel, that's not art. That's the white man's way. Too perfect. A woman can make anything, any kind of shape with her own hands."

As they build up the coils, the potters smooth the clay. Traditionally they used potsherds or pieces of gourd rind for scrapers. Today they use an assortment of coconut shells, tongue depressors, paring knives, wooden spoons, car windshield ice scrapers, discarded eyeglass lenses, can lids and tops from candy, tobacco and aspirin tins. Emma Mitchell at Ácoma jokes that she and her mother and sister have kept Argentine corned beef companies in business because they use so many of their tins as scrapers and trimmers.

The clay has a will of its own, and its shaper must be in tune with that will. Cochití potter Louis Naranjo says, "Sometimes the clay just hides from you. There's a little mystery in it." Blue Corn "does not make a pot just because I like it. I have to make a pot that will like me and looks

Opposite, clockwise beginning at top right—A Santa Clara water serpent pot made by Teresita Naranjo in 1965, courtesy of the School of American Research in Santa Fe; detail of an Ácoma jar made by Marie Z. Chino and painted by Vera Chino, courtesy of Rick Dillingham; detail on storage jar by Lois Gutiérrez of Santa Clara, courtesy of Richard M. Howard; a water serpent plate by Belén and Ernest Tapia of Santa Clara; intricate designs grace a pot by Jody Folwell of Santa Clara Pueblo. Above—Lois Gutiérrez's polishing stones.

selves, too, when we are out of the house. I think the best part, though, is taking it down and finding that it fired good."

Clay, temper, designs, pottery—all are part of being a Pueblo Indian potter. Lillian Salvador of Ácoma says, "It's not complicated to me because that's what was left here for us. I don't know how to describe it—you have to be an Indian to really understand it." Mary Trujillo from Cochití says of traditional pottery: "It has to be that way. Our life is that way."

The potters speak of becoming lost in what they are doing, staying up until two or three in the morning working, preparing for Indian Market. Belén and Ernest Tapia may sand off the polished slip on their red plates six times before they judge it good enough to be sold at market. Santa Clara potter Mary Cain says, "Sometimes I would sit there, busy, busy, busy, and I even forget to come in here to the kitchen and do the cooking for supper. On those days my family excuses me. Then they take me to McDonald's."

Gladys Paquin sometimes yearns for a "regular" job. "My mind tells me 8 to 5 would be a lot easier. My heart tells me different."

Tradition and the marketplace interact. Many potters still pray to Clay Woman before they make their pieces, but they make their living from the work as well. Maxine Toya has "a hard time parting with my pieces; it's part of me that's going, too. Whatever you have put into that piece has helped make you a better person. When you are done and you hold it in your hands, to me, it comes alive."

No wonder traditional potters speak sadly of the increasing use of molded pottery, commercial paints and clays, and kiln firing. Traditional pots simply *feel* different. Even so, some skilled Pueblo potters are beginning to paint molded "ceramics" because they believe they can make better wages by doing so.

Traditional potters can recognize shortcuts because the commercial techniques make the pottery look "too perfect." Though many of them strive for perfection, they always compare pottery to people. Candelaria Gachupín of Zía told her daughter Dora Tse-Pe: "When people have imperfections, do we destroy them because they are blind or deaf or have lost a limb?"

Dora fears, "One day pottery making is going to go. I tell my girls, 'I feel good that I'm helping keeping it going. And I want you to do the same thing.' They are following my advice. And I hope they always will."

Opposite, clockwise beginning at top left—Taos pot by Bernice Suazo-Naranjo; Cora Durand's pottery at Picurís Pueblo; drummer by Mary Trujillo of Cochití Pueblo; unpainted, unfired figures by Maxine Toya of Jémez Pueblo; Taos pots ready for sanding by Bernice Suazo-Naranjo. Above—Ácoma olla by Lucy Lewis made in 1963, courtesy of Richard M. Howard.

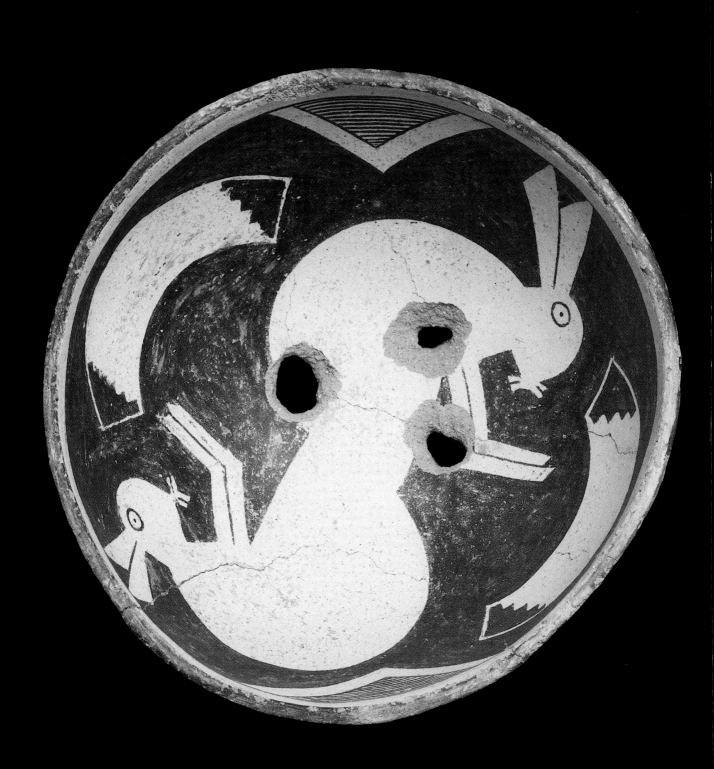

Belief in Life and Continuity
The Mimbres People

The Mimbres River rises in the Black Range of southwestern New Mexico north of Silver City and flows south and east toward the Río Grande. It never reaches there, however, as it sinks into the sands in the vicinity of Deming. North of Deming, where the river was reliable enough, and south of Sapillo Creek, where the growing season was long enough, the Mimbres was home to one of the many small farming groups that flourished in the American Southwest after A.D. 200. *Mimbres* is a Spanish word meaning "willow," and the ancient people who lived along that shallow stream have come to be called the Mimbreños.

Archaeologists today classify the Mimbreños as a branch of the Mogollón culture, a prehistoric group of farming people named for a mountain range that honors an otherwise obscure 18th-century governor of New Mexico. Mogollones lived in southern New Mexico and Arizona, parts of west Texas and adjoining portions of northern New Mexico for about a thousand years following A.D. 200. Their ancestors had lived in the region for millenia, making their living by hunting and foraging in the deserts and mountains of their territory. Even after they turned to the cultivation of corn, beans and squash, most Mogollón groups continued to rely also on the natural environment for game and wild plant foods.

The Mimbreños were in an ideal location for that sort of economic life. Their high and narrow valley is a cool oasis in a hot country. Ponderosa, fir and spruce forests grow above 7,200 feet where winters are too severe and summers too short for agriculture. Below 5,600 feet is the shrub- and grass-covered desert where the river stops and rainfall is too light and the summer heat too intense for reliable food production. The 30- or 40-mile stretch between these two zones was where the Mimbres farmers lived along the cottonwood- and willow-lined stream surrounded by pigmy forests of piñón, juniper and scrub oak. They could farm comfortably within reach of wild foods in the nearby high mountains, temperate woodlands and hot desert. Deer, rabbits, bighorn sheep, elk, antelope, walnuts, piñón nuts, wild grapes, berries, agave and mesquite were only a few of the resources within easy walking distance.

Agriculture and a sedentary life were the key elements of Mimbres culture. At first their settlements were small, no more than tiny villages of only a few houses built high on hills away from the river. Their earliest houses were roughly circular structures called pit houses that were about 15 feet across and excavated into the ground. They had side walls and roofs of wood and adobe, and each one presumably was home to a single family. A village in about A.D. 300 might include 6 to 10 families, perhaps 20 to 50 people. In all, there were only about 500 Mimbreños then.

Later generations moved closer to the river and apparently came to depend more on agriculture. Populations increased, villages grew and housing styles changed. By the Classic Mimbres period from about A.D. 1000 to 1150, there were about 4,000 Mimbreños, and some villages may have been home to as many as 300 people. Houses were of adjoining, aboveground, rectangular rooms, constructed of cobbles and adobe with flat, adobe-covered roofs. Twenty or 30 such rooms were joined together in a single unit, and several room blocks in the larger villages were arranged around a large plaza, as in modern Indian pueblos. Specialized religious structures resembling modern Pueblo kivas were built. Some rooms within blocks were set aside as storing or cooking spaces and a single family probably used several rooms. Groups of related families may have lived in each room block of a village. These later Mimbreño communities were obviously more complex socially, religiously and politically than earlier ones had been.

Mimbreño villages were located as far west as Arizona,

by J.J. Brody
Photography by Mark Nohl

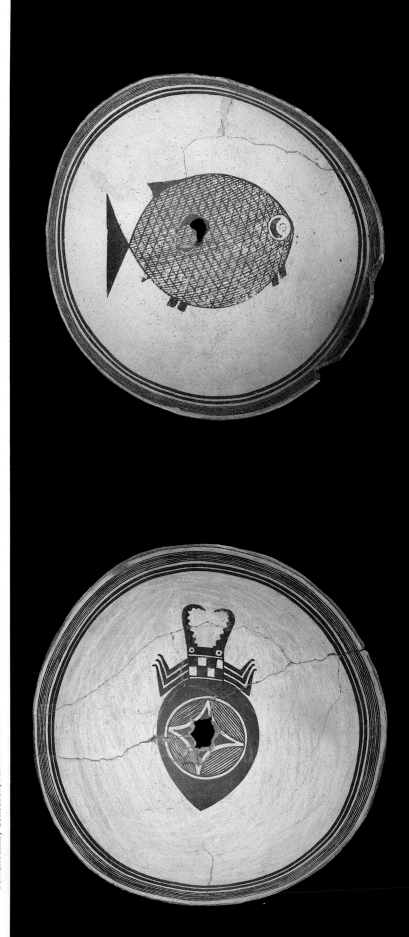

east to the Río Grande and as far south as the border with Mexico. In the Mimbres Valley, no Mimbreño houses were built after about 1130, according to the evidence of tree-ring dating, and the valley was abandoned by 1150. The reasons for the abandonment are not clearly understood, but overuse of resources due to overpopulation seems to have been a major factor, and the other Mimbreño communities were left empty at about the same time. A generation or two later, other farming groups reoccupied the territory, but by 1450 it was abandoned once more. Apaches moved in and were the only native peoples in the region in the 18th century when the first European settlements were built there. Mimbreños were almost certainly among the ancestors of some modern Pueblo Indian people, but there is no archaeological trace of them after about 1150.

The Mimbreños would be no more—or less—interesting than any other prehistoric Southwestern farming people who had no written language were it not for their painted pottery. Their paintings, especially those representing life forms such as birds, insects, mammals, humans and mythic beings, were their hallmark. We know the Mimbreños by their art, and when they stopped making that art at about the time they left their valley, we lose track of them.

They began making pottery at about the time they built their first villages. Most of it, like that of other Mogollón people, was unpainted red, buff or brown ware decorated by texturing rather than painting. They made

All pots shown are Mimbres Classic black-on-white. Holes indicate "killed" pots used in burials.

32

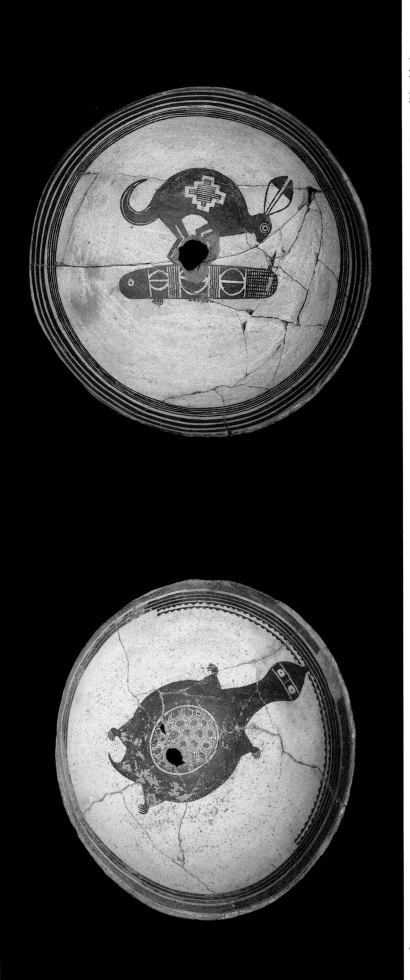

School of American Research Collection, Museum of New Mexico

many different utilitarian forms, including large, wide-mouthed storage vessels, small, globular cooking pots and miniatures of all sorts.

They first painted pottery in about A.D. 700 in a style similar to the painted wares made to the west and south by other Mogollones and by the Hohokam people of south-central Arizona. This was a brown ware painted in red with broad brush strokes. An evolution toward fine-line, black-on-white painting began about 750 and matured about 300 years later with the style we call Mimbres Classic black-on-white. As early as the 800s, their black-on-white paintings were distinctive, as was the ware we call Mimbres Boldface, using designs of such life forms as lizards and birds derived from the Hohokam. However, that painting style emphasized tightly controlled lines and small-scale design units that suggest an aesthetic system related to that of the Anasazi people of the Four Corners region.

It is difficult to know how these visual resemblances should be interpreted, as they can draw attention away from the truly unique qualities of Mimbres pottery paintings. Those qualities transcend subject matter, design and style, permeate the very fabric of the pottery and are related to the way in which much of it was used.

Most Mimbres pottery paintings were applied to the smoothly slipped and polished interior wall surfaces of bowls. These are remarkably unlike their exterior surfaces, which are unslipped, unpolished and barely

School of American Research Collection, Museum of New Mexico

smoothed. Bowl interiors, then, were treated as artists' canvasses. That these vessels were used as art rather than as containers is confirmed by the many thousands of Mimbres pots buried with their dead that show no other use than service as funerary pottery.

About 10,000 Mimbres pottery paintings are known today—the Maxwell Museum at the University of New Mexico in Albuquerque has photographs of about 7,000. Yet, so large a proportion of Mimbreño paintings was buried with their dead that the art was virtually unknown in its time outside of Mimbres territory. The Hohokam and some nearby Mogollón neighbors knew of it, for sherds (but few whole vessels) have been found at some Hohokam and Mogollón sites. But only a handful of Mimbres sherds have been reported from the hundreds of contemporary Anasazi sites excavated and reported.

Most painted Mimbres pottery was ritually "killed" by being smashed or having a hole punched in it at the time of burial. Usually a bowl was placed over the head of the dead person, who could then look eternally into the picture that was painted on its inner surface. Burials were often placed in abandoned rooms or in adobe-lined pits dug below the floor of rooms still occupied by the living. Similar metaphors stressing the continuity of life and death, of past, present and future, characterize Mimbreño art. Lines are tense and are joined to make shapes filled with black paint. But the black shapes often define other white forms in the unpainted slip, and either black or white can be read as the "real" visual message. Duality, ambiguity and harmony made by the tense balance of oppositions are everywhere: black and white, positive and negative, movement in and movement out, to the left and to the right, all are in balance, all are the same.

Things pictured in Mimbres art are rarely what they seem at first glance. A geometric design may be a flower or a cosmic map showing the four world quarters, the zenith and the nadir both in the same center space, which may also be the middle place as in Zuñi legend. The belly of a rabbit may be a crescent moon, men may have animal heads or a bear, human limbs. A rabbit may have the tail of a rattlesnake or a man the body of a fish. Even the most mundane scenes— men trapping birds, gambling or fishing— may depict events in a mythic world as well as in this one. It is a mortuary art made for both the living and the dead, for both occupy the same space.

Animals are usually shown in a void framed by a line that may be the horizon or a ground line. Often alone or in pairs, animals occasionally interact as though they were characters in a story, active in a real-world space. Thus three-dimensional reality is sometimes suggested in these flat paintings by perspective drawing, stance, posture, attitude, interactions and relative proportions. This is a complex art made with only a few simple parts and practiced by only a few artists in any village. These were subsistence farmers and, for all of their skill and invention, the Mimbres pottery painters

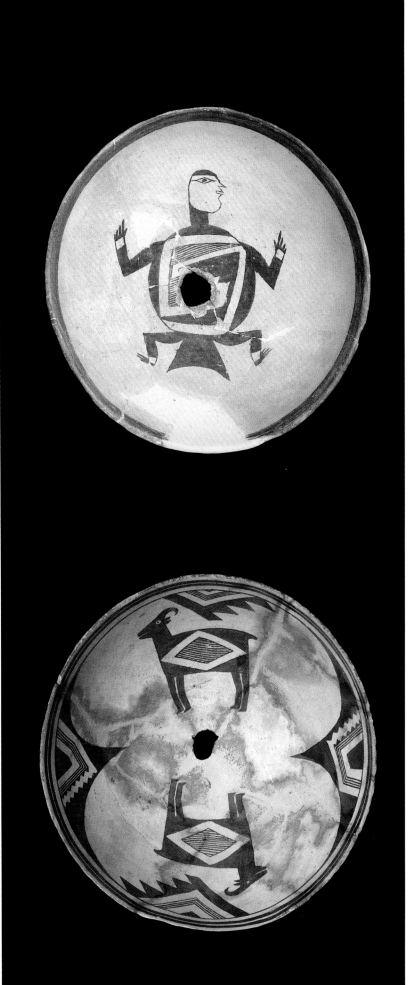

Mimbres Foundation, Maxwell Museum

Museum of New Mexico Collection

could not have been full-time specialists: practiced, trained, thoughtful, but never professional artists in a modern sense.

Out of world view for 750 years, Mimbres art was rediscovered in the late 19th century by soldiers and ranchers casually excavating in the Mimbres Valley. Some became more interested and built collections; others, such as Hattie and Cornelius Cosgrove of Silver City, became professional archaeologists. A half-century ago the outline of Mimbreño prehistory was drawn by the Cosgroves, Wesley Bradfield of the Museum of New Mexico and Paul Nesbitt of Beloit College. More recently it has been refined by the work of Steven LeBlanc of the Mimbres Foundation as well as others, including the late Charles Di Peso of the Amerind Foundation and amateur archaeologists such as Mary and John King of Hurley. The scientists and amateur archaeologists work against time and the threat of commercial looters who mine Mimbres sites in order to feed an avaricious art market. Mimbres art has become a valued commodity, and greed now threatens all Mimbres sites as well as our ability to learn more about these people.

Aptly, Mimbreño mortuary art represented life and continuity, rebirth and the future even as it commemorated death and the past. In about 1924, Julian Martínez of San Ildefonso Pueblo saw pictures of Mimbres pottery in a scientific publication. He adapted some of these and painted them on pottery made by his wife, María. One of these designs, the feather fan, is now a hallmark of Tewa pottery. A few years later, potters at Ácoma also adapted Mimbres designs to their work, and Mimbres art has thus been integrated with that of a Keresan Pueblo. Mimbreño artists continue to make their mark.

Indian Jewelry
Two points of view

"Wen I was a little boy, and Indian Market was just a small sale at Fiesta time, I remember we would go in to Santa Fe the night before and find ourselves a good spot under the portal [of the Palace of the Governors] and sleep there all night," says Cippy Crazy Horse. "You had to do that to save your spot."

"I never heard of Indian Market until I started doing sil-

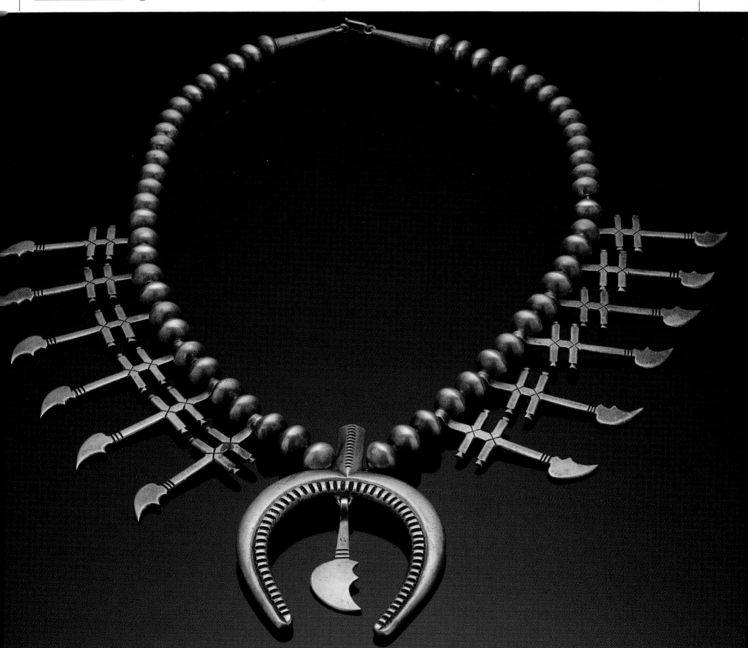

by Kate McGraw
Photography by Mark Nohl

verwork, and that was only several years ago," laughs Richard Chávez. "But now it's a part of our lives. It was responsible for my first real break."

Indian Market for these two outstanding young artists—Crazy Horse of Cochití Pueblo and Chávez of San Felipe Pueblo—is a thread that connects their successful careers and the generations of their families. When they talk about Indian Market, their comments reflect their own perspectives. Chávez, the contemporary silversmith, sees the marketing possibilities. Crazy Horse, who works in more traditional styles, sees a family history. The two artists agree, however, on the importance that the yearly event has for them. It is one of the great markers in the seasons of their lives.

Crazy Horse and Chávez also have in common that they both grew up in pueblos and live in their home villages and that they each came to the work that has bloomed into success relatively late in their twenties, after trying other careers. Other than that, the only thing they share is a transcendent joy in their work. They are really more different than alike, almost polar opposites of one another. Their divergent paths illustrate the freedom afforded successful Native American artists today—the freedom to be themselves.

Cippy Crazy Horse was born Cipriano Quintana in Cochití Pueblo. He is a tall, robust man in a T-shirt and overalls, his long black hair pulled back in the traditional wrapped style for Pueblo men. Crazy Horse, who changed his name several years back, is a witty, loquacious man who laughs often. "I changed my name because I thought it sounded too Hispanic, and I was wearing a beard at the time—well, as much of a beard as I can manage—and people would question whether my jewelry was Indian," he says with a chuckle. "So I asked my dad, and he said to go ahead, that he'd often thought of changing his name himself, and we were out in a pasture where this old horse was kicking up his heels and being silly, and someone said, 'Look at that crazy horse,' and I thought that would make a good silver stamp signature using the letters CZH for Crazy Horse, so I decided to become Cippy Crazy Horse," he explains in a typically nonstop sentence. "I only found out later that it's a famous name in Indian history; we didn't learn anything about Native American history when I was growing up."

Nor did Cippy learn much about the art of jewelry making, although his father is Joe H. Quintana (JHQ), a well-known Cochití silversmith, and his late mother was a fine designer. For Cippy, the road home was a long loop: first, he wanted out of the pueblo. He went off to Eastern New Mexico University for two-and-a-half years and then joined the Navy to see the world. He saw it, too—Paris, London, the Mediterranean, the Caribbean . . . and the more he saw, Cippy says, "the more I appreciated our life back home. What we have."

He did bring one import home: his wife, Sue, a non-Indian whom he met in her native Connecticut while he was stationed with a submarine fleet in New London. Or, as he explains deadpan, "I ran an ad in *Mother Earth Magazine*: 'White woman wanted on pueblo,' and I was about to give up when she showed up with all her luggage on her back at my doorstep, so I had to take her in. And she's pretty good to have around, so I've kept her." Sue, who has put up with this nonsense for nigh onto 18 years, just grins.

The couple has two children, Erly Ann April ("She was due in May"), and Moses ("What other name would you give a boy who's going to go through life with the last name of Crazy Horse?"). Erly is into horses and being a teenager, her father reports, but Moses is already showing an interest in silversmithing. "I know it looks like everything's scattered around in my workshop, but I know where everything is, and I always know when Moses has been in here, 'cause all the tools are moved and the stamps are messed up," Cippy says with affectionate exasperation.

Moses shows a great deal more interest than Cippy did in *his* father's work. Even after he returned to Cochití Pueblo from the Navy, he wanted to work "in a modern job" and signed on as an electrician's assistant on the construction of Cochití Dam. But when someone dropped a heavy light

Right—14-karat gold necklace and earrings by Richard Chavez. Lapidary work is lapis lazuli and coral with turquoise accents. **Above inset**—Contemporary bracelets of silver and 14-karat gold also by Richard Chavez. Stones are lapis lazuli and coral, with turquoise accents.

Cochití Pueblo artist Cippy Crazy Horse (above) fashioned prize winning necklace (previous page) in a traditional Isleta cross design.

fixture on his foot and leg, that ended his electrician's career. Today, though Cippy is officially 35 percent disabled, "I just walk slow and nobody knows," he says with a laugh.

Back in 1979, it wasn't so funny. Cippy and Sue had a baby to support and the workmen's compensation wasn't stretching very far. He decided maybe the family trade wasn't so old-fashioned. A man could do it sitting down. "I learned by myself, step by step, although my parents encouraged me. I started making silver chains, and with the money from that, I bought more tools," Cippy says. Almost from the beginning, collectors and gallery owners were aware that a new and original artist had arrived. Cippy realized at 30 that he had inherited his father's renowned silversmithing touch and his mother's design ability. Today, he has outstripped Joe H. Quintana on the commercial market, showing in the prestigious Dewey Galleries on the Santa Fe Plaza. "The Deweys kind of gave me the big break, and I'm grateful to them," he says.

Like his father, Cippy works in the old style with very traditional, very simple Pueblo designs. He is especially well known for his deep cuff bracelets of solid silver. "We still do it the old way, melting silver down into ingots and making our own tools from scraps," Cippy demonstrates. "Of course, we're not fanatics; I doubt that our ancestors had acetylene torches," he adds with a chuckle. And he still consults with his father, who lives around the kiva from his house.

"I go show him work I've done that I think it's so original and he says, 'Oh, sure, I did that 30 years ago,' and it really gets me," Cippy says with a mock glare. He taught himself copper enameling, with his dad's help. His sisters have learned the process, too. And Cippy is working harder than ever at living a full, well-rounded pueblo life. Although he gripes constantly that he's too busy to get all his orders filled on time, he adds in the next breath that he thinks this year he'll put some alfalfa in the pueblo fields he's allowed to till, and maybe some traditional vegetables in the next field. He has served as one of the pueblo officers, and although he grouses gently that "once they call your name, you can't turn it down; you're stuck," the obvious truth is that he was proud to serve in the office. "I grew up here, and now I'm getting old and I'm interested in learning, in trying to learn and help keep up the pueblo traditions," he explains in a rare solemn moment.

For Richard Chávez, south of Cochití at San Felipe Pueblo, the old traditions are observed on feast days, but he also lives in the modern world. Chávez grew up in a very outward-looking family, he explains: "We were always encour-aged to get an education, get out, get into the mainstream." For a while, Richard managed to leave, attending high school at nearby Bernalillo and then Fort Lewis College in Durango, Colo., for a year. That's where he met Sharon, his Hopi-Tewa/Navajo wife. The two transferred on scholarship to the University of New Mexico (UNM), but even with Richard's part-time job as a draftsman for a local architect, they were having a hard time making ends meet.

Richard's only relative who made jewelry was his grandfather, who showed his college-student grandson how to make turquoise heishi necklaces. "I started with that in 1973, and for the next three years I worked, went to school and sold heishi at trade fairs around the area," Richard reports. "It finally reached the point where I was cutting class to make jewelry—I had started experimenting with silverwork and semiprecious materials in about 1976. So in 1979, I decided to quit school and do it as a career."

It was a conscious, very deliberate decision, as are all of Richard Chávez's choices. A slender man in an immaculate shirt and designer jeans, his hair cut into a smooth, modern style, Chávez could fit neatly into any upwardly mobile setting. His studio—not a workshop, he corrects gently—which he built back of the house, is the opposite of Crazy Horse's dirt-floored, chaotic den. A person could have an emergency appendectomy in Richard's studio without a qualm.

"I'm sort of obsessive," Richard says apologetically, re-

Right—San Felipe Pueblo artist Richard Chávez created this contemporary choker necklace of 14-karat gold and lazulite.

Richard Chávez fashions metal in his studio.

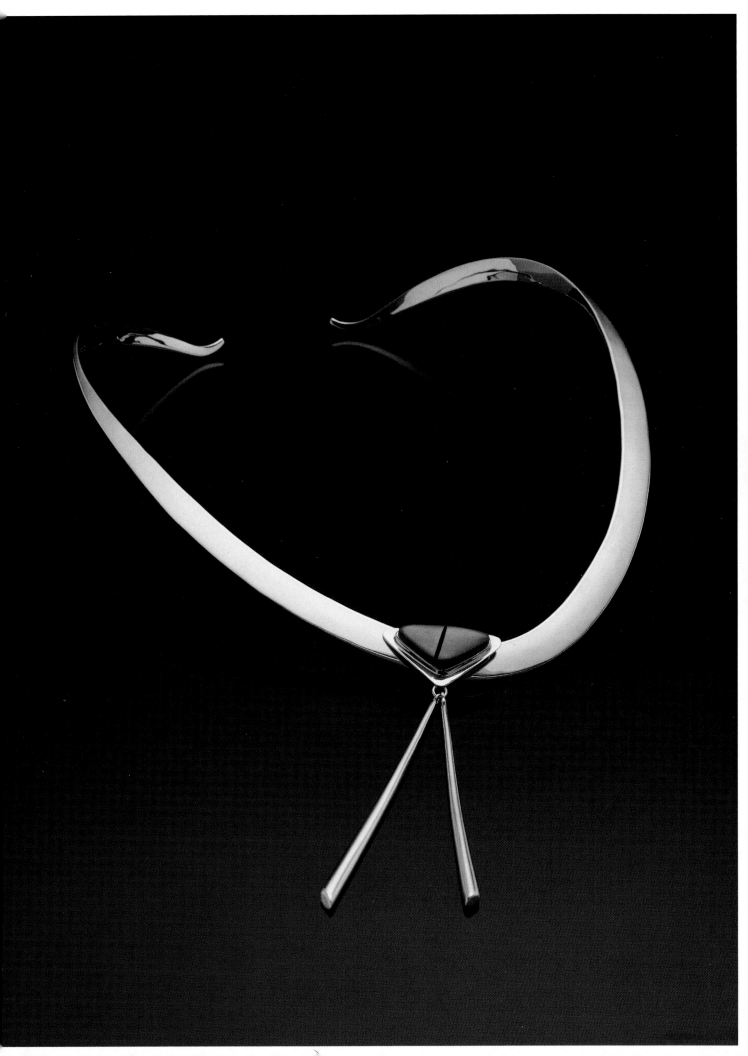

Opposite—A traditional necklace of silver beads encircles a turquoise and silver ring. **Above inset**—Traditional silver bracelets. **Below**—Traditional silver belt buckles and concho belt. All jewelry on these two pages by Cippy Crazy Horse. Crazy Horse pounds his silver jewelry from one-fourth-inch thick silver ingots.

flexively straightening a tool that is imperceptibly out of line. "But it really does get messed up some. When I'm working hard on an order, I let it get messed up. But then once the order is done, I have to come back and spend a couple of days cleaning everything up again. I just can't work in confusion."

Although he never heard of Indian Market until he started making jewelry himself, Richard is a fast learner. In 1976, he showed his jewelry at Indian Market for the first time. Sharon brought the items he was entering to Santa Fe, and when she returned to pick them up for the booth, they were gone. Frantic, she searched them out. "She found them at the prize booth," he said, "with a big ribbon on top—it was a set I'd made—but even then, I didn't fully understand. I had no idea what that meant in real terms," he adds with a chuckle. He soon found out. The award meant the set sold almost immediately, and so did his other items. Even more important, the Indian Market win introduced him to a whole panoply of monied collectors and dealers.

"I started traveling, getting business," he says. "My first showing was with Martha Cusick in Chicago. She came by the booth at the 1977 Indian Market and purchased some things and asked if I wanted to do a show at her gallery. I was so green, I really didn't know what she meant. So I committed myself to doing a show, got some pieces done and showed at the Indian Tree Gallery in Chicago. It really was successful, and more important, I learned quite a bit about what was involved in doing a gallery show successfully, how to talk to people and so forth," Richard says.

Learning is another of his obsessions. He is a self-taught artist, who says he learns new metalworking skills the same way he learned the basics: "I got a book about it and taught myself." In 1981 the Southwestern Association on Indian Affairs, the organization that sponsors Indian Market, awarded Richard a $2,500 fellowship to develop his jewelry-making techniques.

Richard's work, which is shown at Packard's on the Santa Fe Plaza, uses inlaid bands of lapis lazuli, onyx and sometimes turquoise and coral in silver and gold settings. His abstract style is constantly evolving and was influenced mostly by his one-time architectural leanings, he says. "The man I worked for, Harvey S. Hoshour, worked with Mies van der Rohe, and he really showed me a lot about good design. His philosophy was 'less is more,' of course, and I think it's mine. I worked for him for three years, and that's definitely enough time to be influenced by somebody," he says with a smile. "I started out wanting to do traditional, but I just couldn't see myself in it. I started experimenting

with the designs and experimenting with the stones, and I started seeing things I liked. About the third year, about the time I started showing my work, I had my certain style, and from there it started getting more and more refined."

Richard says not much of his Pueblo Indian background has influenced his art. "I never felt comfortable associating that with jewelry," he says quietly. "Jewelry is an art form and that's as far as it goes; I don't put a lot of symbols into the jewelry because I've always felt uncomfortable with that."

However, he does feel comfortable at San Felipe Pueblo. He and Sharon and the children—Cynthia, Alissa, and Jared James—returned to the pueblo a few years ago to restore and live in his parents' 37-year-old adobe house. With careful remodeling, Richard has rebuilt the home into a spacious, modern dwelling that fits neatly into its riverside landscape. "It's so nice and quiet here; we were so conscious of the noise in Albuquerque and Dallas," he says. He has done most of the construction work on the house and studio himself, as well as all of the design. "It's my recreation; it really refreshes my mind," he says.

Like Cippy Crazy Horse, Richard looks forward to Indian Market. Like Cippy, he doesn't know how many "really special" pieces he'll have for competition, or whether the pressure of his successful career will forfeit the time for making those pieces. But he anticipates with pleasure having his own booth, meeting old friends and showing his work. For both men, the purist and the stylist, Indian Market is rapidly becoming a family tradition they're proud to pass on.

14-karat gold rings by Richard Chavez. Lapidary work on man's ring is lapis lazuli and coral.

Partners in Art and Life
Gail Bird and Yazzie Johnson: master jewelers

Yazzie Johnson and Gail Bird.

The partnership of Gail Bird and Yazzie Johnson, the master jewelers whose contemporary concha belts have won numerous awards at the Santa Fe Indian Market, extends far beyond making jewelry together.

Partners in life as well as work, they are one of those magical couples for whom the whole is greater than the sum of its parts.

Gail, a Laguna-Santo Domingo Pueblo Indian, and Yazzie, a Navajo, have been collaborative jewelers for 18 of the 21 years the couple have been together. Gail designs the big contemporary pieces and Yazzie fabricates them.

The same dovetailing happens in their private life. Gail plants lilacs, Yazzie plants fruit trees and together they tend a large vegetable garden.

When you talk with them, sipping tea at a long pine table in their cool adobe house, Gail is gregarious and chatty; Yazzie more laconic. But then you realize that it's Yazzie whose dry wit is providing the punch lines to Gail's stories.

For instance: They spent their teens together, attending the Inter-Mountain School in Brigham City, Utah, where her mother and his parents were teachers and counselors. But that's not where they met, explains Gail.

Gail Bird is the only girl of four extremely artistic and productive siblings. Her brothers are Charlie Bird, a jeweler; Larry Littlebird, an actor and filmmaker; and Harold Littlebird, a potter and poet.

Gail and Yazzie met when Charlie brought Yazzie home to Laguna Pueblo for some hunting one fall. Yazzie was 15; Gail was 12; and it was she, bundled into warm jacket and jeans and stocking cap, who tagged along with them.

"I thought it was great that Charlie had a gunbearer," Yazzie drawls.

He didn't dream the gunbearer was a little sister instead of a little brother until she took off the cap. Says Gail, "My long, thick braids fell out. He just looked at me."

That first meeting was not noticeably intense, despite Gail's crush on Yazzie. The truth is, he ignored her—"There is a big gap between 15 and 12," she concedes.

The gap had narrowed by the time she was 16. They discovered they liked the same music, laughed at the same jokes. They liked to talk together and (Gail at least) liked to write letters.

"By the time I was nearly 20, we just sorta ended up together," she concludes.

From the other end of the table comes a gentle laugh.

by Kate McGraw
Photography by Mark Nohl

Left—Coral and garnet necklace with a clasp of agate and silver. **Middle**—Chinese turquoise and silver. **Right**—Black onyx, hematite and Montana moss agate necklace with a Botswana agate clasp.

"That sounds like the romance of a lifetime," says Yazzie. "We just ended up together."

Gail is a small, compact woman. She has a warm smile, what are possibly the largest doe-like eyes on the planet and an innate elegance, even in chinos and a camp shirt.

Yazzie is medium-tall, classy-slender, with a benevolent humor in his fine-boned face and a trademark long, black ponytail of hair.

Now in their 40s, the couple live in a "modern" ("That means it has indoor plumbing," says Yazzie) adobe in the upper Río Grande Valley near Ojo Caliente.

Gail and Yazzie came to this house on a complicated, winding trail. Their life together started in 1969, when they were attending college in Berkeley, Calif. That year, they decided to move to Santa Fe.

For three years in Santa Fe, Gail baked for a local caterer and Yazzie did construction work. Together they worked part time in an Indian arts gallery.

They began learning about jewelry by studying the pieces in the gallery and reading the books the owner lent them. "I learned about making jewelry by handling old pieces," Yazzie says.

They took off for more college for two years, returned to New Mexico and found the house in Ojo Caliente. They planned to stay only a year, but Gail and Yazzie have lived for 13 years in the thick-walled adobe with strong vigas.

"It took us three years to save up the down payment after we decided to buy it," Gail says, and Yazzie comically be-moans the joys of home ownership—"the new roof, the re-wiring. . . ."

But they love it and admit they could not live as happily elsewhere. The couple have settled in comfortably to its big common room, two studio spaces, a bedroom and kitchen.

They have no children but share their home with two dogs and two cats. They are also raising chickens and turkeys on the property.

Back in 1972, when Gail and Yazzie decided to return to college, they were awarded scholarships to the University of Colorado at Boulder. The pair still needed money for the move to Boulder, and Gail's brother Harold had a booth at Indian Market in Santa Fe that August.

Little did they know they were beginning a career as jewelers.

"I figured I would just make a simple concha belt and sell it from Harold's booth and that would bring in enough to move us to Boulder," Yazzie recalls. So he did that.

("Typical of Yazzie," comments Gail. "Most jewelers would start with a few rings and bracelets. He started with 'a simple concha belt!'")

Yazzie and Gail had faith in their artistic talents. Gail was then, as now, a designer, but Yazzie considered himself a sculptor. "It's still an interest of mine. Sometimes I buy large stones, but mostly I just look at them," he says self-deprecatingly.

It was pure economic necessity that motivated the pair's jewelry making, but they approached it with typical Bird-

*Top left—Silver bracelet with coral. **Top right**—Bracelet with Chinese turquoise. **Below**—Traditional silver bracelets.*

Necklace and earring set, made of gold, charolite and holly agate.

Belt (private collection) made of silver, coral, turquoise and lapis. Belt buckle made of silver and Owghee jasper.

Johnson-like thoroughness. At the beginning, Yazzie even made his own tools.

They started with traditional designs. Yazzie still makes a lot of traditional rings and bracelets, mostly for sale at their two direct markets, the Eight Northern Indian Pueblos Show at San Ildefonso in July and the Santa Fe Indian Market in August.

Except for contest pieces, the stunning Bird-Johnson contemporary designs are shown and sold at four galleries: Dewey Galleries, Santa Fe; Martha Lanham Cusick, Chicago; Joanne Lyon Gallery, Aspen, Colo.; and Potcarrier, Burlingame, Calif.

Today, collectors and museums worldwide vie for the limited output of concha belts, necklaces and earrings from Gail Bird and Yazzie Johnson. But theirs has been no overnight success.

People may think Gail has an outstanding personal jewelry collection, but she says that's not so. Occasionally Yazzie makes a piece just for her out of sentiment, but "most of my collection is just pieces that the public has rejected for the moment.

"We've found that whenever we go in a new direction, it generally takes a year or so for it to be accepted," Gail says.

Gail and Yazzie began designing and making jewelry for art as well as money while in college. Then as now, they were on their own private cutting edge.

"Our work was rejected by some people as 'non-traditional' because we were using stones like agates and jaspers. In fact the use of unfaceted, polished stones is very traditional for Indians if you go back far enough," Gail says. "And, too, we were working in brass and resisted moving to silver and gold for a long time.

"We've always been very resistant to changing our ideas just because someone else says we should," she adds, almost apologetically.

In 1974, Gail and Yazzie entered Santa Fe's Indian Market for the first time. They didn't exactly make a splash. Until 1979, they sold a lot of Yazzie's traditional pieces (he received several firsts and seconds in the traditional division during this period) but very little of their brass-and-stone work.

In 1979, the couple entered a concha belt of mixed metals and different stones, and the Indian Market registrars didn't know what to do with it—they finally accepted it under "Miscellaneous Jewelry."

It wasn't even judged. "It was a real blow," Gail remembers. "We felt it was the best thing we'd ever done, but nobody else seemed to think so."

"Well, not 'nobody else.' Just the judges," says Yazzie.

"That's true," Gail says. "People kept coming by the booth to look at it, including the Indian artists. I remember we were asking $2,100, and a woman from Texas finally bought it."

Between 1979 and 1980, resistance to their work decreased. In 1980, Gail and Yazzie entered some fairly traditional pieces using jaspers and agates and took a divisional award and the Otero Creative Excellence Award. "It was real

exciting, because it was like the judges finally saw what we wanted to do," Gail says.

Also in 1980, Gail and Yazzie were awarded $1,000 in one of the first Southwestern Association on Indian Affairs fellowships. They used the money to visit Utah and northern Arizona to see major petroglyph sites in the canyons there, because they had been working with designs using the prehistoric pictures.

"We were putting the stones in simple settings to show off their natural beauty and making designs on the back that related to the stones and their context," Gail says. "The pictures we use are animals that might have existed in the environment of the stone—butterflies or birds with the lacy agates, for example."

On their fellowship-funded trip, Gail and Yazzie found evidence of what they suspected—that there is a perceptual style change and sophistication in the petroglyphs of the Ancient Ones.

"We thought, 'Yeah, this is what we've been trying to do,'" she says. "It just pulled it all together for us and made us feel that what we were doing was really right."

In their gratitude, Gail and Yazzie designed and made a belt that was an homage to the SWAIA fellowship called "Petroglyph Migration" and entered it in the Indian Market.

"We didn't expect it to get anything because we'd won the Otero and the fellowship the year before, but it got Best of Show in 1981," says Gail.

"That was quite incredible—to go from being rejected to best of show in two years," Yazzie says. "We really felt like maybe it had come much too early."

Gail and Yazzie now design and make fought-over belts, pendants, necklaces and earrings set mostly in gold and silver. Their latest work uses cast designs as well as incised pictures.

They have grown familiar with a vast assortment of lovely semiprecious jaspers, agates, calcedony, baroque pearls, corals and unfaceted gemstones. The couple have developed, over years of visiting "every rock shop in the U.S.," about four reliable sources for special stones.

"Sometimes I wonder why our galleries put up with us, we put such restrictions on our work," Yazzie said. "We never do anything on commission, we work only in the materials we like, we only do one belt a year—which means that of the two galleries that get belts, they only get a new one every other year. . . ."

Gail and Yazzie don't work on commission because their work is so personal. "Each belt is a culmination of a year's work, the lessons learned in that year," she explains.

The jewelers have made only two belts on request. One was done for a dear friend's 40th birthday. Her husband just asked them to make it personal for his wife.

The other commission was for a collector in Chicago who told the couple, "I don't care what you do, how long it takes or how much it costs."

Yazzie, as usual, had the perfect response. He told the man, "That fits just barely within our work methods."

Carved in Cottonwood

Dolls depict life on the Bisti

The Navajo on the Bisti somehow survive off their sheep, goats and cattle. There are few trees to provide wood suitable for carving in this arid territory of northwestern New Mexico. Johnson Antonio has to cut his cottonwood logs from fallen trees in the washes and riverbeds near Farmington and haul them to his clapboard home in the Lake Valley section of the Navajo Nation. There, alongside a picket fence, Antonio has nurtured his own cottonwood, maybe 12 feet high. The shade under this small tree defines the studio in which the artist works.

The People (a term the Navajo use to refer to themselves) on the Bisti dress for the climate as they have for the last hundred years, in jeans and homespun; they lean into the wind, cover their heads against cold and heat. The harshness of survival is etched into their faces and mirrored in their posture; the religion and customs of the Navajo are unbending in a world of accelerated change. It's the People on the Bisti and their animals that Johnson Antonio captures and preserves in remarkable cottonwood carvings he calls "dolls."

by Chuck Rosenak
Photography by Mark Nohl

By tradition, the Navajo don't carve—except maybe occasionally to copy a Hopi kachina. But Antonio has carved now for approximately seven years, and the art is unrelated to ceremonial use or custom. "It comes from here," Antonio says, pointing to his head. "I never seen any other dolls like mine—not even in books. It all comes from here."

But the art was a long time in developing. In fact, Johnson was more than 50 years old before he began making the sculpture for which he is becoming recognized.

The artist was born on April 15, 1931, five miles west of his present home. Antonio was raised and schooled on the Bisti. He attended Lake Valley School off and on until 1949, but he gave no thought to the study of art.

Then in 1951 Antonio began working for the Union Pacific Railroad. "They picked me up in a bus at the trading post," he remembers, "and took me off to lay steel. It was hard work, and when the laying was done in the fall, they'd take me home again. I'd collect unemployment till they'd come for me in the spring."

Antonio worked for the Union Pacific until the spring of 1974, when "I decided I didn't want to go no more."

Also, by the time he quit laying steel, he was married and began raising a large family. Antonio married Lorena, a Bisti woman, in 1977. The couple have eight children, four girls and four boys. In recent years, the Seventh Day Adventists have built a mission school, La Vida, about a mile from the Antonios, where the younger generation is in attendance. "But I tell you," Johnson said, "if it weren't for the selling of the dolls, I couldn't afford the $15 a semester the school charges for each child."

And so Antonio carves for the money, but he also carves out of a desire to communicate with the outside world, to capture the spirit of the People and their animals. The Antonios understand virtually nothing about the art collectors and galleries buying the work.

Until five or six years ago, when the Vietnam Veterans Memorial Highway between Thoreau and Farmington was completed, Lake Valley was connected to the world by dirt tracks. It was 50 miles over these tracks to the stores in Farmington. It was over this route that Johnson Antonio

Navajo Hunter

fearfully carried his first carvings, wrapped in old cloth in the back of his horse-drawn Navajo wagon, to Indian trader Jack Beasley. Antonio made that journey to Farmington to pick up drinking water in 50-gallon barrels, but he thought that "maybe—just maybe" somebody would give him needed dollars for the dolls. Jack Beasley recognized instantly that the carvings were folk art—something separate and apart from the traditional craft of the Navajo: blankets, pots and jewelry that he had been trading in all his life. He bought them, and Antonio's window to the outside world opened.

"In recent years I began to realize," Beasley said, "that the folk art—the unique and sometimes eccentric expression of the Indian—was not being preserved; only their tribal art and craft were recognized by collectors and dealers. And so I was delighted with the carvings Antonio brought me and agreed to represent him."

Beasley began selling the dolls to dealers in Santa Fe. He also arranged to have the Wheelwright Museum of the American Indian in Santa Fe give Johnson Antonio a show in December of 1983.

The show was a critical success. Galleries in Santa Fe, Phoenix and even Chicago started to exhibit the work of the isolated artist. The dolls found themselves in many important private and public collections, including the Wheelwright and the Taylor Museum in Colorado Springs, Colorado.

As a result of these unexpected sales, the Antonios were able to buy a brand new pickup truck, the family pride and joy. With the completion of the new highway, they now can make round trips to Farmington in comfort.

Despite all of the success, visitors to the Bisti will find life basically unchanged for the Antonio family. Antonio still works in the shade of his small cottonwood, carving the likenesses of the People and their animals—his neighbors. He whittles the dried logs with an old pocketknife and paints the figures with watercolor and gouache. The animals are decorated with uncarded wool, glued to the wood. He sometimes attaches real horns found in the neighborhood to the heads of the sheep and goats, giving them a

Navajo With Baby

Woman With Shawl

Yei Dancer

Red Cow

Smoking Break

Smoking Break

Rabbit Hunter

55

Chuck Rosenak

Johnson Antonio holds a young goat on the Bisti.

realistic appearance.

The art is lifelike to a point, but the perspective of a trained artist is missing. However, these qualities—lack of perspective, the use of unmixed colors—make the carving folk art and add a charm and vitality to the dolls that could not be expressed in any other way. Johnson Antonio's creations are from the heart—from his vision of life around him.

When Antonio sits back late in the day, adjusts the brim of his hat and says, "Lorena, I have finished these dolls,"

Lorena prints his name on the base of each one, as well as a post office box number in Kirtland, a small town where the Antonios receive mail through the auspices of a local Indian trader. They take the dolls off for sale in the new pickup truck to Farmington.

"I don't really make them for sale. I make them for myself," Antonio sighs, "but we need the money. Unfortunately, the cash will soon be gone, but the dolls will last forever." ⚘

Zuñi Bead Dolls
Back in Style

In the '30s, they were everywhere. Beaded curio items lined the shelves of shops throughout the Southwest. Believed neither unique nor valuable, these Indian-made goods nevertheless were bought by thousands of tourists. Beaded figures of Comanche men and women, their furry rabbit feet peeking out from pants and skirts, dangled from ignition keys of countless family cars across the country. Cub Scouts appeared at den meetings back home proudly sporting beaded "cow heads" at the necks of their kerchiefs.

While it's true that these items were inexpensive souvenirs of a visit to Indian country, they were unique. Made by the elder women of a tribe, each beaded figure was painstakingly created as an individual piece.

Although "cow heads," made from sheep vertebrae, and key chains were first made as tourist goods in the early 1900s, beadwork dates back to the early 1700s. According to Rain Parrish, former curator of the Wheelwright

*Comanche on horseback
by Lonita Telese*

Museum of the American Indian in Santa Fe, beadwork came to the Zuñis from trading with the Plains Indians. It was an important aspect of Plains Indian life, and was found on saddles, clothing, cradleboards, moccasins and items used for hunting and warfare. Small dolls and animals made of beads were used as amulets and tied to children's cradles to encourage the good and harmonious.

Today, at Zuñi, in western New Mexico, beadwork is experiencing a revival as many younger women are beginning to create unusual new designs.

Claudia Cellicion, a 27-year-old Zuñi woman, won a first place in beadwork at the Gallup Intertribal Ceremonial last year for her representation of a Hopi Butterfly Dance as a set of figures. The Butterfly Dance also is a social dance performed at Zuñi. This year she completed a Navajo dance scene complete with spectators. And she again won the first place award at the Gallup Intertribal Ceremonial.

Cellicion became interested in beadwork after watching her grandmother-in-law, Lonnie Poncho, make the rabbit-footed Comanche figures. She carves the inner figure of cottonwood, sews a cloth covering over it by hand, and then spends approximately three to four hours attaching the beads to the 4-inch figures.

Eighty-three-year-old Elaine Kanteena is a more typical profile of a beadworker. She learned by watching other women work, and decided to become more serious about it herself about four years ago. Kanteena's daughter carves the core of the figure out of balsam wood, and Kanteena does the rest. She makes her figures 10 inches tall and creates complete Indian dance costumes for them. The process takes about two and one-half days. The dolls resemble those made during the Depression years. Kanteena remembers many of the early traders at Zuñi encouraging the women to do beadwork.

Zuñi women like Cellicion and Kanteena are responsible for creating a growing market for beadwork. Today, many trading posts have a waiting list for the more unique beaded figures. With the popularity of folk art still growing, Zuñi beadworkers expect to enjoy the demand for their work for some time.

by Polly Summar
Photography by Michael Mouchette

*Girl with barrette by
Claudia Cellicion*

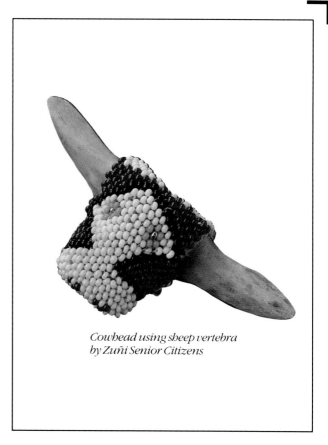

*Cowhead using sheep vertebra
by Zuñi Senior Citizens*

*Two Olla Maidens
by Leonardine Penketewa*

*Navajo Lady
by Claudia Cellicion*

Where Drums are Born
Two Cochití craftsmen carve with patience and pride

It is a blessing, the elders say, to have a handmade pueblo drum in a home. They won't say why. It has to do with the spiritual beliefs of the drum makers.

"Drums are the heartbeat of Indian country," veteran Cochití Pueblo drum maker Bill Martin says. "The people come to the plaza, they come to the feasts or to the ceremonials when they hear the drums."

Individual drum makers are scattered throughout New Mexico's Indian country. Fine drums are made in Taos Pueblo. But the largest concentration of drum makers is found at Cochití Pueblo, midway between Albuquerque and Santa Fe. Some say that is where the best drums are made.

Since the retirement of the venerable Marcello Quintana, Martin is a kind of elder statesman/spokesman for the drum makers of Cochití. He works at a nearby school and focuses his energies on making one or two large drums per year. A drum maker who makes more drums but still clings to the Cochití traditions of quality and craftsmanship is Steve Herrera.

Herrera started making drums only seven years ago, but he uses skills he learned as a child. He turned to drum making after he retired from the Air Force and his farming efforts back home on pueblo land were ruined by seepage from nearby Cochití Dam.

"I was surprised at how it all came back to me," Herrera says. "My wife, who'd only known me since 1954, was amazed. She didn't know I could do that."

According to both Herrera and Martin, the Cochití preeminence in drum making started with the Anasazi, their ancestors, when the ancient peoples lived at what is now Bandelier National Monument. With an abundance of nearby aspen to make drum shells, it was only natural that these forefathers of the Cochití should become the best, they say.

Pueblo people use drums for ceremonials and social dancing, not for messages. The message drums so beloved of Hollywood played no role in Pueblo customs, Herrera says. "The Pueblo people have always stayed together; we

Steve Herrera clings to Cochití traditions in making his drums.

by Kate McGraw
Photography by Eric Swanson

A close-up view of Steve Herrera's carefully crafted drums.

had no reason to send messages by drums. When we wanted to send messages to other pueblos, we sent runners."

Herrera and Martin learned to make drums just as their predecessors have for centuries: by watching and helping the elder drum makers. Martin learned by helping his grandfather Santiago Cordero. Herrera grew up helping his stepfather, Lorenzo Cordero. Both were good teachers. They taught that drum making cannot be rushed. Done correctly, it takes time.

Herrera describes the steps of making a drum today. First, he has to get a U.S. Forest Service permit to cut and remove dead-and-down aspen trunks from the high mountain canyons of the Jémez Mountains—aspen is the only wood the Cochití use. The logs are trucked down to Cochití, cut into cross-sections and left to dry until they are soft and flake-tender in their core. Sometimes it takes a year or more for a big aspen cross-section to dry enough to begin carving.

Above, left—Steve Herrera uses a handcrafted chisel made from a shovel handle and a car spring to chisel out the core of one of his larger drums. ***Above, center****—He uses a chisel and mallet to clean out a smaller drum.* ***Above, right****—In one of the final steps of making a drum, Herrera tightens the lacing of the rawhide around the drum.*

Meanwhile, Herrera acquires cowhides from Cochití farmers and barters with his friend Amos Gaines, a Mescalero Apache, for elk hides left when trophy hunters haul off the heads and discard the rest. Several fine Steve Herrera drums provide a heartbeat at Mescalero Apache ceremonials.

He cleans the hides by soaking them in the Río Grande for two or three days—longer if it's a winter-slaughtered cow because the coat is tougher and thicker. When the hides are softened, Herrera scrapes them with a piece of lumber or a draw knife to remove the hair. Then he stretches them, dries them on top of a shed near his workshop and rolls them.

Next he must start cleaning out the drum shell. He uses a mallet and chisel for most pieces of log, painstakingly chiseling out the core. He must start at the center, clean out a part of the log's core and then set the drum shell aside to dry some more. It can take two weeks to clean out a medium-sized drum shell, but this lengthy, fastidious approach is essential to make sure the wood never contracts and changes the shape of the drum skins.

Once he's got the shell chiseled out, Herrera cleans it with a draw knife or rasp and then sands it. Some drum makers don't bother to clean neatly inside, but "I think it makes a better sound when you take care," he says firmly.

Then he pours warm water into an old, freestanding bathtub in his homebuilt workshop and soaks the skins until they are soft again. Herrera cuts them into rounds that fit the drum shell and laces them to the shell through holes made with an awl. Once laced, the shell dries another two or three days or more, depending on its size. The skins are stained with leather stain or heel-and-sole polish and then sealed with a professional waterproofing.

Herrera paints his own design on commercial drums. He leaves the drums made for other pueblos unpainted so the drummers can paint them with their own colors and designs.

The Cochití artisan rarely sells a drum to an Indian drum group for cash, but he trades for items he wants. He sells commercially at powwows and the State Fair and from his home in the middle of the pueblo. Herrera will not agree to make drums in wholesale lots—"It takes too much time to do it right, and I won't be rushed. I am not a machine." Besides, he says, he likes to know the people who buy his drums. He likes to meet them and laugh with them, including Japanese tourists who are somewhat startled to be greeted by a Native American drum maker who speaks a few halting phrases of Japanese from his Air Force days.

"I tell them not to copy our drums and send them back at us marked 'made in Japan,'" he says with a mischievous laugh.

Imitation drums, drums made with chainsaws and wood that hasn't dried properly, are an increasing concern of the Cochití traditionalists. "I always advise people to know the drum maker, to buy from him and not from some shop," Martin says. Both Martin and Herrera say they have never had a drum returned because it has cracked or the skins have slipped or torn, but they have had drums brought to be repaired that other, more slipshod craftsmen have turned out. They refuse to work on the drums.

The Martin and Herrera drums can both be found at nearby pueblos and even in Hopi country. They can be found in non-Indian homes used as end tables or pedestals for Hopi kachinas. Martin says his drums are in use in schools for rhythmic lessons, in music conservatories, by jazz and rock groups looking for an older sound to include with their own and in hospitals and clinics where they are used in therapy sessions.

Both drum makers also play and sing with their own drums on Cochití feast days. Herrera collects traditional In-

Bill Martin plays one of his drums. He generally makes only one or two drums a year.

dian songs, traveling to powwows and around New Mexico, Arizona and Utah to collect the songs. Playing on one of his drums, he teaches them to his grandchildren.

"Our traditions are not written, like the Constitution or the Declaration of Independence," he says. "They have to be taught, and the songs and the drums are a part of that teaching."

Both men have older sons who have no interest in drum making. "They say they'd rather learn a trade, something that brings home a paycheck, and I can understand that," Martin says. Herrera figures he makes about 30 cents per hour—very minimum wage—with his drums. But both men also have sons and grandsons growing into manhood who *are* showing an interest in the craft, and that gives them great pleasure.

Every drum has a deep-toned side and a lighter-toned side. The deep side is used to call the people to the ceremo-

nial; the lighter is used for the dances themselves. "When I hear one of my drums played, it makes me feel good; it makes me feel like I got a blue ribbon, a trophy or something like that," Herrera says. "The drums don't like it indoors. You have to put them by the fire and warm them up for them to play well. Best is to take them outdoors, where they were born and made. The drums remember the sun and the wind when you play them."

"Something is embedded deep in the drums that sends the message back to you that you should continue," Martin says. "It takes time and energy and it doesn't pay, but the work is its own love and its own reward. Maybe I'm here to provide this craft and to teach the future drum makers."

And maybe that's why a Pueblo drum is a blessing—because it brings into your home the sun and the wind and the aspen and the elk, and perhaps a little of the dignity and grace and patience of its maker.

Warmth With Elegance
The Navajo chief blanket

When the history of our time is written, it is doubtful that the down jacket or the Burberry raincoat will find much space on the pages of textbooks, much less on the fronts of T-shirts or as subjects for artists.

Front and back views of Navajo chief blankets, considered First Phase circa 1800-1860, show the elegant draping effects the blankets give. The use of bayeta *red and indigo blue was one of the first departures from the simple arrangement of brown and white stripes in uniform widths. Silverman Collection.*

by Polly Summar
Photography by Mark Nohl

But deep in the Southwest, the merging of weaving talents between the Pueblo and the Navajo Indians in the late 1600s produced an outer garment that reigned then, and now, with such distinction: the chief blanket. It is a striking rectangular blanket easily identified by bold markings—black and white stripes with patterned accents of red or other bright colors.

The name signifies its stature among both Indians and the white man, but it is actually a misnomer. According to Rain Parrish, former curator of the Wheelwright Museum of the American Indian in Santa Fe, "The prime misconception about chief blankets is that they were owned by chiefs."

There are no so-called chiefs in the Navajo tribal system, but some historians believe the name may have stemmed from various Plains Indian tribes that traded with the Navajos and reserved these striking blankets for their chiefs. The blankets were highly prized by the Navajos and became an important trading commodity.

The chief blanket was the black-diamond mink coat of the era. Warmth, of course, was a consideration. But if it had been the only concern, there were easier ways to make rugged outerwear. Other woven garments of the time were cut and sewn. Admittedly, it would have been difficult to perform those functions on such a heavy fabric, but that was probably not the main reason for continuing to make the chief blanket.

Dr. Joseph Ben Wheat, as curator of anthropology at the University of Colorado Museum in Boulder, described the impact of the chief blanket best, when he wrote: "When displayed flat, it appears somewhat static; but wrapped around the human body, it flows elegantly, and as the body moves, the design becomes as kinetic as mobile sculpture."

The use of gray-brown wool in stripes that are usually white makes this Second Phase blanket unusual. The red color in the blanket, circa 1860-70, is from both commercial red yarn and raveled red fabric. School of American Research, Santa Fe.

The insertion of blocks of red into the chief blanket's wide stripe bands is characteristic of the mid to later 1800s. This Navajo blanket, using indigo blue and bayeta red, dates to 1850-60. Collections of the Museum of New Mexico; gift of Mrs. Harry Kelly, Helen Kelly Kane and Daniel T. Kelly.

The drama of wearing the chief blanket must have made the machinations of draping it worthwhile, for the garment had to be arranged to keep the wearer warm while still allowing enough mobility for walking and moving one's arms. The blanket was usually draped like a cape over the shoulders and pulled together in front. Depending on its design, two focal points were then created: one in the center of the back and one in front as the two half units of the design met.

Although chief blankets today are most often seen on the fronts of T-shirts, a popular tourist item in New Mexico, the regal air of wearing a cape-like garment is still present. Santa Fe Opera-goers still talk about the striking figure cut by artist Fritz Scholder when he donned a flowing black cape one summer's opening night.

Chief blankets actually evolved from garments designed for women—shawls or dresses in narrow stripes of brown and white. The blankets were woven in the shape of a rectangle, crosswise instead of lengthwise, with the warp threads parallel to the short side. The earliest chief blanket that historians know of, a brown-and-white striped loose tapestry weave, was found in a Navajo grave dating to 1775.

The first step toward the chief blankets we know today came when the two brown stripes at the margins were widened. Inside those borders were woven narrow stripes of indigo, which probably reached the Navajos from the Pueblo Indians. Mexican indigo was brought by mule train to the Spanish villages along the upper Río Grande. The other stripes, white and brown, were natural wool colors, with the brown varying in shades from dark to almost black.

Next, the weavers used another wide band to divide the striped field in half lengthwise. Narrow blue stripes were

The red in this blanket has a blue cast and is possibly an early Germantown yarn with cochineal or resinous lac dyes. Purchased from Mrs. Carolene Sheriden Buler 1929; School of American Research, Santa Fe.

often incorporated into that area, too. Then came red, with oblong blocks of that color often inserted in the wide stripe bands. The red was probably *bayeta*, the Spanish name for English baize, a flannel fabric. It arrived in the area via Spain to the New World, where it was used for trading and again, probably reached the Navajos through the Pueblos.

The particular red of the *bayeta* was achieved by dyeing the fabric with cochineal, a dye made of ground powder from the cochineal beetle cultured in Mexico. Then the fabric was cut into strips, unraveled and hand twisted.

From this point on, the design was often determined by the sex of the wearer. In women's blankets, the three wide bands continued to be the theme, while in men's blankets, the bands became secondary to the elaboration of the block designs.

In the blankets of accomplished weavers, the design lines remain true when the corners are brought in to meet at the center and then folded again.

The introduction of yellow was probably the first of the Navajo's native vegetal dyes. The light yellow was produced by steeping peach leaves, and a brighter yellow was made later from flower heads.

Before the introduction of *bayeta* and the native dyes of yellow and green, the colors of red, yellow and green often surfaced in certain old Navajo fabrics. Historians believe, judging from the texture and color shades, that the yarns can be traced to discarded army uniforms that were unraveled and hand twisted: the scarlet red of the infantry, the yellow of the cavalry and the green of the medical staff. The appearance of these colors was brief since the supply was apparently quickly used, and *bayeta* and native vegetable dyes soon followed.

The merging of Pueblo weaving know-how into the Navajo culture probably happened when the Spanish re-

Purchased in 1941 from Mrs. G.W. Challerton in Los Angeles, this Navajo shoulder blanket dates to 1865-75 and incorporates vegetal and native dyes.

turned to this area in 1692, after the earlier Pueblo Revolt of 1680. Entire Pueblo villages fled to live with the Navajos for several years. While Pueblo men were the weavers in the Pueblo culture, Navajo men were accustomed to a life of hunting and battle, and so Navajo women adopted the art.

Weaving became sacred to the Navajos, and there was a religious ceremony for baby girls that prepared them for their future as weavers. In *The Dîné Origin Myths of the Navajo Indians,* published in 1956 by the Smithsonian Institution, the legend has Spider Woman saying: "Now you know all that I have named for you. It is yours to work with and to use following your own wishes. But from now on when a baby girl is born to your tribe you shall go and find a spider web which is woven at the mouth of some hole: you

must take it and rub it on the baby's hand and arm. Thus, when she grows up she will weave, and her fingers and arms will not tire from the weaving."

Today, however, the role of weaving in the Navajo culture is a different one. While still vital to the Navajo's life and economy, it is not considered part of the cycle of life for *every* Navajo woman. Beginning around the turn of the century, an increasingly technological and informational society created inevitable changes.

Chief blankets are occasionally still made today, but the proud Indian man of the 1700s and 1800s would be very surprised to see those blankets being walked on rather than worn.

Hands-on Artisans
Jicarillas keep in touch with their past

The green building along U.S. 64 in Dulce is deceptively sober. Inside is a riot of color.

This is the Jicarilla Apache Museum and Arts and Crafts Center, displaying the work of the tribe's finest artisans.

The Jicarillas are not related to the Pueblos of New Mexico but to the Plains Indians. Their crafts are distinct. Basket weaving and beadwork are their specialties. These they execute with an unerring sense of design and a buoyant use of color.

Fewer artisans work at traditional crafts than in earlier times, but the center is helping preserve the Jicarillas' artistic heritage, director Brenda Julian says.

"These are what I call the manager's special," she says with a smile as she points to a glass case full of baskets and beadwork. "All of these have won ribbons at the State Fair. This shows the finest work and reminds everyone here always to strive for their very best."

The museum's permanent exhibit features sepia-toned photographs of long-vanished Jicarillas, paintings of tribal life, ceremonial costumes and a collection of baskets, some by Tanzanita Pesata, the best-known Jicarilla basket weaver. Contemporary baskets and beadwork also are displayed; many items are for sale.

The artisans work quietly in adjoining rooms. A sense of communal harmony reigns as each woman bends over her task.

Dishes of glass beads form a rainbow on the worktable where Marjorie Gonzales assembles a beaded belt buckle. She is trying a new pattern, she says, as she spears a brilliant sapphire blue bead and stitches it onto the buckskin backing. Others work on small wooden looms, making belts and hat bands.

Beadwork is an old craft among the Apache. Their tradi-

Avis de Jesus works on a basket.

by Gabrielle G. Palmer
Photography by Susan Contreras

tional dress—women's deerskin dresses and moccasins, men's trousers, vests and leggings—are customarily decorated with beaded designs. Though these are still used for ceremonial occasions, the objects of modern trade are more

likely to be necklaces, earrings and bolo ties.

Basket weaving, too, is part of the Jicarilla heritage. Learning this trade from the Pueblo Indians, the Jicarillas soon became skilled at basket weaving, passing it on from generation to generation. Ardella Veneno remembers her training under older craftswomen.

"I asked all kinds of questions," she says. "Why do you do it this way? How do you do that? They always told me. They want the younger people to know, to show their interest. They are proud of their work."

Veneno says she perfected her work through trial and error. "When you first start, you have an idea what the finished basket looks like but you can't do it. It comes out rough and you want it to come out real neat. But if you don't let your interest fade, if you keep working, you get particular about your work and it becomes more and more interesting."

Each artisan gathers the willow and sumac she needs. The materials are gathered from September to April when the plants are strongest. The best basket makers consider every step of the process important. They don't cut just any branch but often go to the heart of the bush, sometimes crawling on their hands and knees, to find the straightest, strongest ones.

Communion with nature is part of the tradition. "Just hearing the river, I feel good," one woman says. Another adds, "As I cut, I say 'I will make you into a beautiful basket.'"

Cecelia Harina shows how sumac is peeled and rounded to make the coils that serve as the foundation for the basket and how sewing splints are fashioned. Shaping these splints to a uniform width not only involves a practiced eye. The artisans, Harina says, must "feel it with their fingers."

They can judge, too, whether the willow and sumac are supple and lively, quickly discarding any that are brittle. It takes control and patience to keep the coils uniform, to make small and rhythmically spaced stitches, to keep the sides of a basket curving evenly and gracefully so that a harmonious whole results.

Each artisan keeps her supply of materials tied in bundles. Nothing is prepared in advance except the splints to be dyed.

The Jicarillas generally use commercial dyes. They prefer bright colors—reds, greens, yellows and dark blues—to make designs that stand out boldly against a background of natural sumac and willow. Patterns can be abstract—triangles, stars and stepped diamonds—or stylized forms taken from nature, such as butterflies, deer and flowers.

"The designs are in your head," says Veneno. "Before you start a basket, you think about it. The designs are all there. . . . All the ideas come within."

She adds, "If you get tired of baskets for a while, then you do beadwork. But whatever you do, you have to put your whole mind on it, your whole self and your whole interest in it. Then you get it back."

Visitors are welcome at the Jicarilla Apache Museum and Arts and Crafts Center. The center is open from 8 a.m. to 5 p.m. seven days a week with the exception of holidays. For more information on the arts and crafts center call 759-3515.

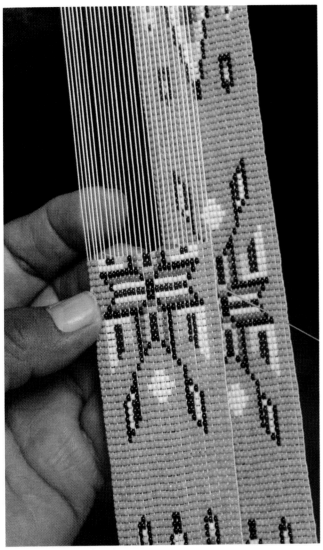

Camelia Elate uses her beadworking skills to make a headband.

A collection of award-winning work made by the Jicarilla Apaches.

Grace Maria and Louise Pesata proudly display Apache tray baskets they are making.

Weaving the Big One
Sisters' determination, traditional skills produce history-making tapestry

Weavers Barbara Teller Ornelas, left, and Rosann Teller Lee spent almost four years creating the largest contemporary Navajo tapestry on record.

by Patricia Guthrie
Photography by Mark Nohl

Rosann Teller Lee refers to it simply as the "big one," as in "I still can't believe we made that big one."

Indian art collectors, such as Sande Bobb, refer to it as "an absolutely exquisite work of art that has gone down in history."

It is 1987's Santa Fe Indian Market Best of Show—a 5-by-8½-foot Two Grey Hills Navajo tapestry that left viewers gasping and judges awestruck, confirming the Teller family as a frontrunner in Navajo weaving techniques. The piece is the largest contemporary Navajo tapestry on record and it netted a record selling price. A Texas businessman shelled out $60,000 to its creators, sisters Rosann Teller Lee and Barbara Jean Teller Ornelas.

For four years, the two worked away on the piece in Newcomb, their hometown in the northern reaches of the Navajo Reservation, a town that lies between Shiprock and Gallup. The tapestry grew ever so slowly—about 3 inches a week—even though they plugged away at it for as many as 10 hours a day.

The project was halted many times: both sisters went their separate ways to bear sons, while arguments over color and other matters strained family relations. But, in the end, it was the entire Teller clan that contributed to the tapestry's finely tuned perfection.

"My dad would come in every day and ask: 'How many inches did you girls get today? How far are you now?'" Rosann remembered at a family gathering in Newcomb. While father Sam Teller built the loom for the huge rug and sacrificed his tool shed for a work area, their mother, Ruth, kept a keen eye on the pattern's straightness and symmetry.

"There was one time she told us we made a mistake, and we had to go back and unravel 6 inches," Barbara recalls. "It took us one and a half days to take out the mistake and three weeks to reweave it." Rosann adds: "We cried so many times over that. I don't think anyone would have seen it, but she saw it."

While each rug off the respective looms of Ruth Teller and her daughters has a unique design, perfection and discipline are consistent patterns in their art, as well as their lives.

"Our mother always made us be busy," Rosann says fondly, looking over at her mother, dressed in traditional Navajo skirt and blouse. "We were always working, cooking, washing, preparing the wool. Before I was 5 and went to school, I had already learned how to cook and weave."

Rosann, the eldest of five children, had the added responsibility of watching over her two sisters, Barbara and Linda, and two brothers, Ernest and Earl. Barbara spent her days with her sisters under Newcomb's cottonwood trees carding and spinning wool.

They watched their grandmothers, Nellie Teller and Susie Tom, their aunt Margaret Yazzie and their mother weave and gossip at their family home behind the Two Grey Hills Trading Post, just outside Newcomb.

Inside the trading post, their father, Sam, sold rugs for 31 years. He was there when the Two Grey Hills style emerged—born out of a trader's suggestion to use natural colors and a unique pattern. The design has become a Navajo rug classic. Collectors treasure it and weavers around the sprawling 16-million-acre reservation copy it.

"A lot of people from the East would come in and tell us they came from across the country to see the two gray hills," Sam, wearing his Boston Celtics cap, explains. "They are right behind the trading post. The two diamond shapes in the rugs represent the two gray hills."

A slight man, Sam has a ready smile and likes to recall the early years when it took two days to travel 60 miles south to Gallup on a horse and wagon.

His wife, Ruth, remembers the days when weavers tried to outwit the traders with sand and rocks—Navajo rugs were sold by the pound, so the heavier, the better. "Mom says they used to try and weave rocks into the rugs, but the traders got smart to it," Barbara says, laughing.

Ruth was known for her rugs by the time she was in her 20s. Although she was forced to drop out of school by the sixth grade to herd the family sheep, she added to the family income with her rug sales, putting her youngest daughter, Linda, through college.

Today, Ruth is grandmother to eight. She still weaves as many hours a day as her eyes will permit, and her rugs net between $2,000 and $6,000, depending on size. Rug buyers manage to find her in out-of-the-way Newcomb; she installed a telephone to make it a bit easier. Although she can speak English to adequately scold her grandchildren, Ruth relies on her native language to express herself.

"She's really proud of us," Barbara says, interpreting for her mother. "She says she never expected weaving like this. It's worth it that she taught us."

Barbara's husband, David Ornelas, a Hispanic from Phoenix, Ariz., is one of the Tellers' biggest fans. While he encourages his wife to take chances, to weave new styles and bold colors, he also respects the traditions of Navajo weaving that evolved from warm blankets to rugs for tourists to a fine tapestry form. He sees, as many others do, that the art of weaving is fighting for survival in Navajo land. Looms compete with video games and VCRs. In Rosann's living room, her loom rests near the color television and VCR.

"Why was it so important for you, *shima,* that you taught

73

your daughters to weave?" David asks his mother-in-law, using the affectionate Navajo term for mother. Ruth smiles at the question as if the answer were obvious. As a girl, she had watched her mother, Susie Tom, weave, and it was only natural she teach her daughters.

"The younger ones are not weaving and I am afraid it will die," she says in Navajo. She turns to her three daughters and granddaughter, Sierra Nizhonni Ornelas, at the dining room table of Rosann's home. "That's why I talk to you all the time about it. Don't lose it. Keep it going."

Her youngest daughter, Linda, who lives in Colorado, says her weaving is "a sore subject" within the family. "I've done some weaving and I've won some prizes. But, I can't sit still like my sisters. I have one rug that's been on the loom three years now, and it's only 5 inches long."

"Just wait till she has kids," Barbara jokes. "Then she'll want to sit still and weave."

Sierra, who is Barbara and David's daughter, is trying her best to carry on a family tradition, but she tends to make a face when asked about her weaving. "I've got my own rug on the loom, but it's got cobwebs on it," says the youngster. "When I get mad at it, I quit."

Both Rosann and Barbara have managed to weave their rugs around the demands of husbands, children and jobs. Rosann has driven Newcomb public school buses for several years and raised three sons with her husband, Larry Lee.

When completing the "big" tapestry, she sat at the loom in between her 5 a.m. and 2:30 p.m. bus duties. With her part of the $60,000 check, she bought a double-wide mobile home and furniture. She hopes to earn enough from her next rug sale to buy a car for her son Larry, who is at the University of Arizona.

While she's weaving, Rosann thinks about "which bill it will pay off, what clothes I can buy for the kids." She markets her rugs mostly through Ed Foutz, the Shiprock Trading Post owner who suggested Rosann weave something "different"—a large tapestry. It was an idea that's changed reservation weaving, the Navajo rug market and the Teller family.

Living in Tucson, Ariz., with her husband and two children, Barbara is successfully marketing her own work. With the money from the "big" sale, Barbara is putting David through Pharmacy College at the University of Arizona. Her skill took her to London to give a presentation at the British Museum, and she was artist-in-residence at the Heard Museum in Phoenix from 1986 to 1987.

Pulling out a scrapbook with photographs of his wife's weaving demonstrations and work, David talks about Barbara's work. "I view my wife as an artist. I tell her to pursue her art form and not to hold back. You have to take a chance and be bold."

Barbara admits her ideas are not always popular. She points to a photo showing a rug with a string of turquoise stones dangling out the edge. The turquoise strand represents the spirit line—the thread guiding the weaver's spirit through the rug. "Some people weren't too crazy about that," she says. And when she tried pastel hues in her Two Grey Hills rugs instead of the traditional browns, grays, and black, she was told she was making "Miami Vice" Navajo rugs.

Following the tradition of their relatives, the Teller sisters are on the cutting edge of Navajo rug creations. Says Santa Fe rug dealer Sande Bobb, the Tellers' 1987 showcase piece "piqued the interest of Indian art collectors everywhere. They may have been aware Navajo weaving existed before, but they thought of it as a curio item. Now, they see this as an art form."

Bobb says the Teller sisters use yarn that is extremely fine—its strands are thinner than dental floss. "It is almost like linen. The yarn is so finely spun and woven so tight that the piece was translucent. You could hold it up to the light and see your hand through it."

A Navajo tapestry is woven tighter than the traditional Navajo rug. To be considered a tapestry, the weft count must be 80 threads per running inch. The Teller tapestry consisted of 95 to 108 weft threads per inch.

The quality of Navajo tapestries is frequently compared to Persian rugs, says Bobb, who runs Santa Fe's Cristof's gallery with her husband, Bill. But the price tag on the Navajo work still catches buyers off-guard, she adds. "Right now I have a tapestry by Rosann the size of a placemat. It is a magnificent Two Grey Hills selling for $14,000. At the same time, I have a huge Ganado Red 7-by-10-foot floor piece also for $14,000. It's a wonderful example of the differences in style."

A Teller original rug seldom gets to stay in a Teller home. As Sam puts it, the only rug of Ruth's in the house is "the one on the loom. Maybe when we get ahead, we'll keep one."

Although their work is netting them record prices and catapulting them into weaving history, the Teller sisters continue to speak of their art in sentimental, not economic, terms.

"It's kind of lonely if you don't have a rug on the loom," Barbara reflects. "Like now, I just finished one yesterday. It's going to a doctor in Brooklyn."

"It's hard to part with it," she explains. "I like to know where my rugs are going. I like to know if they're getting a good home. Each rug is like giving birth to a child. You watch it growing up and when it's finished, it leaves home. Except the rugs don't come home for Christmas."

Animal Dances of the Pueblos

The year is 1822, the scene is Santa Fe Plaza, where people are celebrating Mexico's independence from Spain: "The Peccas Indians came into the city, dressed in skins of bulls and bears . . . they looked like the animals which they counterfeited so well that the people fled from the square," wrote Thomas James, an eyewitness.

The year is 1983, the Jémez Pueblo Plaza: On this day, Jan. 6, descendants of the Pecos Indians, now living with the Jémez Indians, are still performing animal dances, costumed as game animals, eagles and hawks.

All of New Mexico's Pueblo Indian villages present some form of animal dance. The imagery of the dances is unforgettable with the beautiful costumes, the figurative choreography and the dedicated singers. Performed during the year are at least 30 or more—Buffalo, Deer, Elk, Mountain Sheep and game animal dances. The latter includes a mixture of animal and bird disguises. It is often called a Buffalo Dance because the buffalo dancers are the central figures.

Animal dances are rituals, petitioning for the general well-being of the people and animals. They are a portrayal of the bond between the people and the game animals who furnished their food and clothes. Even though disguised as animals, the dancers often carry lances or bow and arrows, blending aspects of the hunted with the hunter. In some dances the animals try to escape. They may be killed and then ritualistically revived by touching them with an arrow.

Our list of animal dances begins in the fall and continues through the winter months when most of them are held. However, the increasingly popular Buffalo Dance may be seen at any time of the year. Some of the animal dances are performed on fixed dates. The rest are usually performed on winter Sundays. The actual date of a dance is not

Deer dancers at San Juan Pueblo.

Text and photography by Luke Lyon

firmly known until about a week before the performance. To find out where they are being held, ask Indian arts-and-crafts vendors in Santa Fe and Albuquerque, call tribal offices or just tour the villages looking for activity. Remember, times are approximate.

OCT. 4: Nambé Pueblo has an Elk Dance every seven to eight years; it was held in 1964, 1972 and 1979. There are four or five elk and about 20 side dancers. 11:00 a.m.

NOV. 12: Some years on this date Tesuque has a Deer Dance with about 40 dancers. Dawn and 11:00 a.m.

CHRISTMAS SEASON: Cochití has Buffalo, Eagle or game animal dances on Christmas and following days. Jémez usually has game animal dances on Dec. 25 or 26. Isleta, Sandía, Santa Ana, Zía and Tesuque may have animal dances from Dec. 25 to 28. At San Felipe, Mass is at midnight on Christmas Eve, and animal dances are held in the nave of the church by three or more dance groups. Mass starts at about 3:00 a.m. at Santo Domingo on Dec. 25, followed by animal and other dances in the church; the dances continue in the plaza until midafternoon. At Taos a Deer Dance is held every other year in the afternoon of Christmas Day.

JAN. 6: On Three Kings' Day most Pueblo Indian villages honor their new officers with a dance, usually some form of an animal dance that starts in midmorning. In 1983 at Jémez, both the Squash and Turquoise groups alternated with game animal dances. Each group had two buffalo, a buffalo woman and about 40 deer, 10 mountain sheep, 15 eagles, two hawks, three antelope, seven drummers and 50 singers. On that same day, Cochití was doing an Eagle Dance.

JAN. 22-23: San Ildefonso celebrates its feast day with a game animal dance (Buffalo) and a Comanche Dance. The North-Side group performs the animal dance in odd-numbered years and the South-Side in even-numbered years. On Jan. 22, vespers start about 6:00 to 7:00 p.m., followed by a procession, animal dance and songs—all illuminated by bonfires. At dawn (7:00 a.m.) of Jan. 23, drummers and singers call the game animals out of the hills to the east of the village. The Game Priest and the hunters lead the animals past the assembled villagers. The animals are dusted with sacred meal. They move to the plaza and dance for a few minutes, then retire to their house. Dancing resumes about 11:00 a.m. in front of the church and continues in the plaza at intervals throughout the day. The number of dancers varies year to year from 20 to 60: two buffalo, a buffalo woman,

hunters, deer, mountain sheep, antelope and side dancers. The male side dancers wear headdresses with one large buffalo horn on the right side.

FEB. 2: Candlemas Day celebrations at San Felipe start at dawn as armed hunters herd the animal dancers out of the hills to the east of the village. Mock kill-resurrection rites are held. The animals and hunters go to the plaza and start dancing about 9:00 a.m.

FEB.-MARCH: On several Sundays there will be dancing at one or more of the Indian villages. The following animal dances seen in 1983 were held in the middle of the day, but Deer Dances begin at dawn. San Juan, Feb. 20: The Deer Dance started at dawn and continued in the afternoon with 102 deer, two Apache clowns, drummer and singer. At the end of the last dance, the deer tried to escape, but they were captured by the villagers and escorted home. Santa Clara, Feb. 13: A game animal dance, also called the Deer Dance at Santa Clara, started at 6:50 a.m., with the animals coming out of the hills to the west of the village. They danced in the plaza for a few minutes. Dancing resumed at 11:00 a.m. There were four buffalo, four buffalo women, four mountain sheep, four antelope, 49 deer, 20 singers and a drummer. Cochití, Feb. 13: The game animal dance had two buffalo, a buffalo woman and a dozen or more deer, mountain sheep and antelope. And on Feb. 27 another dance group at Cochití had two buffalo, two buffalo women, eight deer, four mountain sheep and four antelope. Santo Domingo, Feb. 27: The game animal dance had a white buffalo, two buffalo, two buffalo women, two deer, five mountain sheep and four antelope. The 150 singers wore face paint, roach headdresses and Plains Indian costumes. These were just a few of the animal dances held in the early months of 1983. Actual dates will vary in any given year.

JUNE 24: A Buffalo Dance has been part of the feast-day Mass at San Juan since the mid-1970s. Besides dancing in the church, the buffalo lead the procession of the santos to the bower in the dance plaza. Mass at 10:00 a.m.

AUG. 12: At the 1983 feast day of Santa Clara Pueblo, one of the four dances was a Buffalo Dance and another was a Mountain Sheep Dance. 11:00 a.m.

SEPT. 19: The feast-day celebrations at Laguna Pueblo usually include an Eagle Dance and sometimes a Hunting or a Buffalo Dance. Noon. Photography of animal dances is usually permitted for a fee only at San Juan, Santa Clara, San Ildefonso, Nambé and of special Indian

Jémez Pueblo Eagle Dance.

Buffalo Dance at Santa Clara Pueblo.

dance groups when they are dancing off reservation.

Buffalo and other game animals were an important part of the Pueblo Indians' livelihood. In 1583, the Spanish explorer Antonio Espejo said of the Río Grande Indians, "They dress in white and colored mantas, and tanned deer and buffalo hides." From as far away as Zuñi Pueblo, expeditions to hunt the buffalo were formed. According to Lt. John Gregory Bourke, a buffalo hunt in the 1830s was described by Pedro Pino, famous 19th-century governor of Zuñi Pueblo: "We have no buffalo here . . . . They live on the Pecos. Once I went over there to hunt them. It was a very long time ago, before the Americans came into this country. The Comanches didn't fight anybody then. We left here. There were 50 from Zuñi. On our way to the Río Grande 40 Mexicans joined us. We had a great many ponies, some had 5, some had 6 and one or two had as many as 10 or 11. It took us six days to get to the Río Grande and five more to the Pecos. We went far down the Pecos and out into the Llano Estacado, where there was a stream in a deep canyon. We killed the buffalo this way. We waited until they came to water . . . . Then we sent a boy on horseback to frighten them. They came running up the side of the canyon . . . . We ran up among them and lanced them in the side behind the shoulders. They had drunk so much water and they had had such a hard climb . . . . We dried a great deal in the sun . . . . We stayed in the country 31 days."

The Zuñis still venerate the buffalo. Two mounted buffalo heads decorate the altar area of their restored mission church, and at intervals they do a Buffalo Dance.

Wearing animal-mask costumes and imitating animal movements was and still is a part of religious practices of many diverse ethnic groups scattered around the world. A mural painting of a Reindeer Dance costume, dating from Upper Paleolithic times, is on a cave wall of Les Trois Frères near Ariège, France. The Starr Carr mask in the British Museum depicts a hunting dance around 7500 B.C. in North Yorkshire. The Abbots Bromley Horn Dance, held in the midlands of England in early September, is perhaps one of the few remaining game animal dances in Europe. Six reindeer dancers, a hobbyhorse, harlequin clown, a man-woman figure and musicians appear in the Horn Dance—all characters similar to those seen in New Mexico's Indian dances.

The animal dances of the Pueblo Indians, however, are undoubtedly among the greatest in number and variety of any surviving in the world.

Tablita Dances of the Río Grande Pueblos

Santa Clara Tablita, Nancy Hunter Warren

F rancisco Vásquez de Coronado once observed, "The water is what these Indians worship, because they say that it makes the corn grow and sustains life." It was Aug. 3, 1540, and Coronado was at Zuñi Pueblo searching for gold in the fabled cities of Cíbola. Though he was wrong about the gold, he was right about the Pueblo Indians venerating water and corn.

Today the Pueblo Indians continue their prayers for water and corn in several types of elaborate dance dramas: Corn Maiden, Blue Corn, Yellow Corn and the often-performed Tablita Dance, also known as the Corn Dance. The Pueblo Indians devote more than 25,000 dancer-hours (number of dancers times hours of performance) to Corn Dances each year, with an estimated 35,000 dance watchers in attendance.

The Tablita Dance is named after the distinctive headdresses made from a thin board (*tabla* in Spanish) worn by the women dancers. In the 1800s, this dance was known as the Baile de la Tabla, Dance of the Tablets. It has different names in the various Pueblo Indian languages. Many English speakers began calling it the Corn Dance; and to add to the confusion, it is also called the Green Corn, the Harvest, the Saint's Day or Feast Day dance. At Hopi a similar ceremony is called the Butterfly Dance.

The origins of the Tablita Dance are obscure. During the rapprochement of Spaniards and Indians following the 1680 Pueblo Indian Revolt, however, the Tablita Dance became an acceptable ceremony to the Spaniards, replacing public performances of kachina dances. In the 1600s, the Spanish clergy violently opposed the masked kachina dances, and the dances went underground in the Río Grande Indian villages. Today only at Zuñi and the Hopi villages are non-Indians permitted to see masked kachina ceremonies. The Tablita Dance became a fixture of Indian celebrations associated with dates in the Christian ecclesiastical calendar, including the feast days of the patron saints the Spaniards assigned to the villages.

The symbolism, songs and prayers of the Tablita Dance ceremony petition for rain and for good crops in general, and only sometimes is corn specifically mentioned. The ceremony has wide religious meanings; in the broadest sense, it deals with weather control and with fertility and well-being for all peoples.

Whatever its name, the Tablita or Corn Dance is performed repeatedly throughout the year and is most often seen in the saint's day celebrations. These celebrations are communal, involving practically all the villagers. The days before the public ceremony are devoted to practicing dance steps, rehearsing old and new songs, preparing costumes, baking bread and collecting food for the feast.

Saint's day celebrations start with Mass in the pueblo's Catholic church. The image of the patron saint *(santo)* is carried in procession and placed in a temporary bower of tree branches in the village plaza. In several villages, the

by Luke Lyon

Luke Lyon

A form of the Butterfly Dance was introduced to Santa Clara Pueblos by a Hopi-Tewa who married into the Pueblo.

first dance is held in front of the church before the festive day of dancing in the plaza.

In most pueblos, the people are divided into two kiva groups or moieties. Each has a complete set of dancers, chorus and drummer. The two groups alternate performances through the entire day—perhaps there is a short interval in the early afternoon for the feast.

The Tablita dancers form two parallel lines, men and women arranged one after the other in each line. On the major feast day in a number of the Río Grande pueblos, the dancers follow a distinctively decorated banner, carried aloft on a 15-foot pole. This first part of the dance is a double-line march, either a countermarch or a counterclockwise circuit of the plaza. The dancers in each line are roughly arranged according to height, taller and older dancers at the head and children at the tail. In the second

At Santa Clara, Green Corn dancers assemble atop the kiva while Harvest dancers finish. **Above**—*Children on the kiva steps at San Ildefonso Pueblo.*

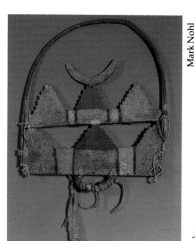

Mark Nohl

Jémez Pueblo tablita, c. 1880, in the Museum of New Mexico Collection.

part, the two lines face each other, the head of one line facing the tail of the other. They either dance in place or interact with the opposite line in complicated movements. The double-line march and the head-to-tail formation are approximately of equal duration; a complete dance of the two parts requires about 25 minutes.

The male dancers wear a white ceremonial kilt embroidered in red, green and black; turquoise and shell jewelry; rain sash; fox skin; colored bird feathers in their hair; and a bandolier of olivella (olive) shells. A gourd rattle is in the right hand, a sprig of fir in the left. In most cases, the men in a particular dance group have the same color body paint. The women wear their distinctive tablita headdresses, black mantas with woven red belts and turquoise jewelry. They carry sprigs of Douglas fir in both hands. Depending on the village, they may be barefooted or wear moccasins.

The chorus follows the drummer as he moves down the plaza during the double-line march. The songs are in the native language. The older men of the village form the nucleus of the chorus. They are colorfully dressed, wear concha belts and carry sprigs of fir. Their gestures are symbols, illustrating the rain clouds; downward motions with lowered palms, followed by horizontal sweeps, symbolize the rain falling on the fields. Other gestures denote the village and the people and express thanks. In the head-to-tail formation, the banner is adjacent to the chorus and is waved over the dance lines as a blessing. Ritual clowns, when present, are nominally in control of the dance lines and the crowd of watchers.

At the end of the first dance, the dancers pay homage to the santo in the bower, leaving candles, money or loaves of bread. At day's end, the santo is carried in procession back to the church.

During the last 100 years and especially the last 30 years, the number of participants in the Tablita Dances has increased dramatically. From 80 dancers at Cochití in 1882, the number grew to 300 in 1983. Santo Domingo had 160 dancers in the 1880s and 784 in 1983. The number is perhaps greater now than at any time in the past, paralleling the growing Pueblo population. The Indian population in New Mexico as a whole has doubled since 1960.

The similarity and proliferation of ceremonies among the many Pueblo villages is a product of sharing and borrowing. As an example, one of the forms of the Hopi Butterfly Dance is derived from the Tablita Dance of the Río Grande Pueblos. It was probably introduced into the Hopi villages when Tewa Indians migrated from the Santa Fe area to Hopi after the 1680 Pueblo Revolt. Now the Butterfly Dance, with its elaborate tablitas, is performed in many of the eastern villages. In particular, a form of the Hopi Butterfly Dance was introduced in the last few years into the Tewa Pueblo of Santa Clara by the Hopi-Tewa who married into the village—the dance has made full circle in 300 years.

The name Butterfly Dance is currently applied to several different dances; e.g., the Santa Clara Blue Corn version has more than 100 dancers; another dance group at Santa Clara performs a Butterfly Dance with about 20 dancers and different choreography; and San Juan has a Butterfly Dance with four dancers and no tablitas and Zuñi performs a Butterfly Dance as one of its social dances. Thus the confusion in dance names continues.

Early references to tablitas and the Tablita Dance are scarce. Polly Schaafsma's *Indian Rock Art of the Southwest* documents prehistoric ceremonial use of evergreens, mantas, stalks of corn, kilts, banners, masks and complicated headdresses—one or two might be called tablitas. Canyon de Chelly has a rock art painting, probably from the historic period, of a mask with a tablita. It is similar to that in use today by the Hemis Kachina, who appears at the Hopi Níman (Home) dances.

Fray Francisco Atanasio Domínguez, in his 1776 inspection of New Mexico, noted, "The women put on some little painted boards trimmed with a few feathers and latticed with agave fiber."

On Aug. 19, 1849, Edward Kern sketched a dance he saw at Jémez Pueblo, later printed in the *Simpson Report*. By the time his observations passed through the hands of Lt. James H. Simpson, lithographers and editors, the drawing had the title of *The Green Corn Dance*. Kern's sketch of the Jémez dance may or may not be what we now call a Corn Dance. However, since it was labeled *The Green Corn Dance*, Lieutenant Simpson's report introduced the name to New Mexico.

Lt. John Gregory Bourke, United States Army, and artist Peter Moran saw the Dance of the Tablet at Santo Domingo Pueblo on Aug. 4, 1881. Bourke published his description of the ceremony in the first chapters of his *The Snake Dance of the Moquis of Arizona,* illustrated by Sgt. A.F. Harmer—who was not present. We do not know why Moran did not illustrate Bourke's book. However, Moran's incomplete but nevertheless excellent sketches of the Santo Domingo Dance of the Tablet are now a part of the Clinton P. Anderson collection at the Roswell Art Museum.

Adolph F. Bandelier saw the Baile de la Tabla at Cochití on Easter, April 9, 1882, which lasted three days. He described the choreography and number of dancers and gave the Keresan name of the dance.

Several writers in the 1890-1920 period, including Bandelier and Father Noel Demarest, suggest that tablitas in earlier times had been made from scraped hides, usually buffalo, but as yet no archaeological evidence for this has been found. Kachina masks, however, have traditionally been made from cloth and hides.

Dance watchers will take special memories with them after seeing Tablita Dances at each village: Aug. 4 at Santo Domingo, the magnificent singing and the numbers of dancers and watchers; the first dances around 11 a.m. on Aug. 2 at Jémez Pueblo, with the staggering number of religious and folklore symbols seen with the dancers: Pecos Bull, hobbyhorses, ritual clowns, santos, Christian cross; the finale on July 26 at Santa Ana Pueblo with two sets of dancers and choruses, church bells, clowns, hobbyhorses, Tcapiyo (the masked supernatural disciplinarian), the villagers carrying the santos and singing "Santa María, Madre de Dios."

The earliest photographs of the dance were apparently taken in the 1880s. Today, photographs of the Corn Dances can be taken—with permission from officials—only at the Tewa villages of San Ildefonso, Santa Clara, San Juan and Nambé, and perhaps some years at the Keresan village of Laguna.

Luke Lyon   Joe Hedrick   Gail Russell

Green Corn Dance (left and center). Harvest Dance (right), all from Santa Clara Pueblo. The old tablita (above) is Hopi, dates from around 1890 and is in the School of American Research Collection, Museum of New Mexico.

83

Corn Maiden in the Cloud Dance at San Juan Pueblo.

Matachines dancers from Santa Clara Pueblo wear one version of dancers' headdress and scarf mask.

Joe Hedrick

The Matachines Pole Dance
Christmas Day at Taos Pueblo

The lively music and bright swirl of ribbons of the Matachines Dance are usual in several northern pueblos on Christmas Day, but only at Taos Pueblo—in alternate years—can you see a variation that Anglos call the "maypole."

In Mexico it is called the *danza de cintas* (ribbons), or *de cordones* (strings); in New Mexico some musicians use the words *la trenza* (the braiding) and *la tejida* (the weaving) to describe the dance their music accompanies. The name used by Florence Hawley Ellis, the dance *de las fajas* (belts), is descriptive of the streamers used by the Taos matachines, and seems suitable for this event.

These belts or sashes are of woven wool, varying in width from 3 to 5 inches, some more than 6 feet long, with braided fringe at each end. They are predominately red, with black, white and green introduced in making designs. Two of these belts are tied together to form a single streamer, then 12 of these doubled bands are fastened to the top of a pole.

The pole itself is 14 or 15 feet high, a straight young tree trunk with the bark removed. This is held upright in the center of the dance area by three or four men. It may be in the plaza or in the church yard, and the 12 matachines who have been dancing take their positions around it, holding the ends of the sashes in their left hands, which also hold the *palmas*.

The matachines dancers of Taos wear regular dark trousers, long-sleeved shirts and vests or sleeveless sweaters; a fringed shawl folded in fourths is fastened to the shoulders and hangs down the back.

The headdress, often referred to as a miter, is typical of the upper Río Grande matachines. The basic form is a solid headband with a stiff front piece about 12 to 14 inches high. This front piece is straight at the bottom, where it crosses the forehead, and curved at the top. It is usually covered with velvet and decorated with many pins and ornaments of silver and turquoise; in some cases, rhinestones and sequins provide more glitter. A frill of satin ribbon, 2 inches wide, outlines the sides and top, and a strip of black fringe, beaded or silk, is attached across the forehead, covering the eyes.

The cluster of bright-colored ribbons falling from the peak of the headdress down the back of the dancer to below his knees creates a very festive look. There may be six or eight ribbons, from 1 to 4 inches wide, fastened to the crown in such a way that the head of the wearer is completely covered. This apparently solid front and back of the headdress leads to the description of being miter-like, and some viewers have assumed a religious connotation.

A final touch to the costume is the square silk scarf, folded diagonally and worn bandit style across the nose and past the ears, where it is attached to the sides of the front piece, with the two ends being tied in back, over the ribbons and the other two ends hanging down over the face, bib fashion.

Each matachin wears gloves and carries a *palma* in the left hand and a rattle in the right. The *palma* is a carved wooden object in the shape of a trident, used in some parts of the complete Matachines Dance as a fan with a waving

by Flavia W. Champe

movement, or in other parts in a threatening manner as a weapon. In 1970, the handle of the *palma* was held in a scarf, and some dancers even had a matching scarf for the rattle. The rattle is covered with a scarf and is held in the palm of the right hand with the points of the scarf hanging out between the thumb and first finger.

It has been difficult to notate the steps and patterns of the dance in an accurate manner. The following description represents observations made of six performances between 1958 and 1979.

La Tejida or the Pole Dance of Taos

Music: 4 measures of 4/4 time.

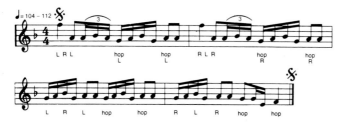

The music was taped in 1960 by John L. Champe with Adolfo Frézquez playing the violin and Claudio Montoya the guitar. The transcription was made by Robert Beadell of the University of Nebraska Music Department.

Basic Step: Moving forward, or turning in place.

Measures	Counts	Steps
1	1 & 2	Step L R L
	3 4	Hop L two times, R foot raised forward
2	1 & 2	Step R L R
	3 4	Hop R two times, L foot raised

Positions of Dancers.

Three or four men, some wrapped in blankets, support the pole in the center of the dance area. The 12 matachines, each with the end of a streamer in his left hand, position themselves in a circle around the pole.

Dance Routine.

Measures

Steps

1-4	Wait
5-8	All do two basic steps turning in place to left, holding left hand with sash over head.
9-12	All do two basic steps turning in place to right, left hand still holding sash over head.
13-etc.	Continue basic step moving forward in weaving pattern.

This weaving pattern, as determined from observation, is made by one group of four dancers moving clockwise in the circle, e.g., every third man, such as numbers 3, 6, 9 and 12. The other group of eight men moves counterclockwise. The woven pattern develops on the pole as the four men pass their streamers over two of the others, and under the next two, as the groups circle the pole in two directions.

When the streamers have been woven an accepted distance down the pole, or the dancers reach a certain position, on signal, all the men do the basic step two times turning in place left, two times turning right and the music stops.

After a short waiting period, the music resumes, the dancers do two basic steps turning left and two turning right. Then they continue the basic step moving forward as they cautiously reverse their directions, watching carefully as the streamers unwind.

The only time I have ever heard applause during a Matachines Dance was at the successful climax of the unwinding of the pole at Taos on Christmas morning 1979.

Left—*Pole Dance in the Plaza of Taos Pueblo.* **Below** —*Taos matachin dancers have begun to weave the streamers around the pole.*

Basket Dance, San Juan

Easter in the Indian Pueblos

The spring Christian observances of Lent and Easter coincide with Indian ceremonies that honor the awakening spring season, as the days get longer and preparations are made for planting. Christian beliefs, springtime invocations for plant and human fertility, the transmission of the gift of life, are all celebrated with dance and song in the Indian Southwest.

Such celebrations are widespread. The Tarahumara villages, located on the flanks of the Sierra Madre Occidental of Mexico, have processions and dances by entities called pharisees. In the Yaqui communities in Mexico and Arizona, matachines, deer dancers, and *fariseos* perform during Holy Week.

However, the largest number of Easter dances can be seen in New Mexico's Río Grande villages.

The variety of dances that might be

by Luke Lyon
Photography by Joe Hedrick

Harvest Dance, Santa Clara

Spring Dance, Santa Clara

Corn Dance, Santa Clara

Rainbow dancer, Puyé

seen at Easter in the Tewa villages is impressive: Buffalo Dances at Santa Clara; Yellow Corn, Parrot and Butterfly dances at San Juan; and Buffalo, Corn Maiden, Basket, Bow, Footlifting and Spring dances at San Ildefonso. On Easter afternoon, several Indian villages located along an arc from Jémez to Cochití have Tablita Dances. These dances may continue for four days through the Wednesday after Easter. Farther north along the Río Grande, the Tewa villages celebrate Easter with a number of planting season and animal dances. The songs, gestures and choreography abound with native religious symbols.

There are so many choices of how and where to celebrate Easter among the Río Grande villages that visitors—who are welcome in the churches and at the dances—can be reduced to a state of perplexity. The dilemma: where to go to Mass; what dances to see; whether to rush from village to village and risk just missing dances at each place, or stay put in one place and miss the ceremonies at the others.

At Jémez, San Felipe, Santo Domingo and Cochití, the Turquoise and Squash groups each perform the Tablita Dance, a dance with many other names; Anglos call it the Corn, Saint's Day or Harvest dance. Spanish names for it include *Baile de la Tabla* and *Pascua* (Easter) Dance. In the Keresan villages it may be called *ai'ya-shtio-kutz;* at Towa-speaking Jémez, it is *pakwa kish;* and in the Tewa villages, *xoxeye.*

At Santo Domingo, the children of the two dance groups perform on Easter Sunday, but during the next three days the adults dance, accompanied by koshare and kwerana clowns. The female dancers wear headdresses of decorated boards or tablets. There can be as many as 200 children performing this dance at Santo Domingo and about 500 adults during the following three days. At San Felipe there are more than 300 tablita dancers, and at Jémez about 200. San Felipe and Cochití have, at times, continued their Tablita Dances for the three days following Easter.

Over the years the Tewa villages have presented a number of different Easter dances. The Tewa dances have been performed by groups of anywhere from 15 to 80 dancers. They are well rehearsed and the costumes are remarkably consistent in detail.

San Juan usually has one dance group performing, but some years they do not dance at Easter. Although San Juan Pueblo has presented the Parrot and the Butterfly dances on previous Easters, recently they have danced the Yellow Corn Dance, *xotseyinshare.* Equal numbers of men and women, 60 or 80 total, open this dance with the beautiful and impressive *wasa*—or weaving—dance formation. The men sing to the beat of a drum. No matter the direction or the evolution, the dancers use the step called *antege*—accenting and stomping the ground with the right foot. Groups of four dance side by side. The groups zigzag laterally to each other, as the entire formation slowly moves through the dance plaza.

The song changes and the dancers about face and continue weaving, backward and sideward. As the song repeats, they face forward and continue the *wasa* formation. At the conclusion of the song, the dancers line up shoulder-to-shoulder, men and women alternating, in a single dance line. The older dancers and the best singers stand in the center of the line, with the drummer just behind them.

The song begins and they dance the antege in place. The dances are repeated in two more dance plazas. During the afternoon the Yellow Corn Dance is performed four times. The wasa formation is danced only at the first and last performances. The use of the single-line formation, with the male dancers singing as they do the antege right-foot stomping step, is a holdover of the masked Kachina Dance choreography, still to be seen in the masked Kachina Dances in the Zuñi and Hopi villages.

At San Ildefonso Pueblo, the North-Side and the South-Side groups almost always present two different dances on Easter Sunday. The North-Side group frequently does the Corn Maiden Dance, *pogonshare,* at Easter—sometimes referred to as the Rainbow Dance. There are 25 to 30 male dancers and two female dancers. This dance is repeated four times during the afternoon; however, a dif-

Deer Dance, Santa Clara

ferent group of women may perform in each set.

The dance begins with the *wasa* formation, with one woman in a front group and the other in a back group. A line formation follows with the women located within three positions of either end. During the dance, the women step forward from the line, face each other, dance toward and pass each other, then reverse and return to their places. The antege step is used throughout the Corn Maiden Dance, and the male dancers sing to the beat of a single drum.

The Basket Dance, *tunshare,* is also often performed at San Ildefonso Pueblo at Easter time. In the South-Side version, four small evergreen trees form a square with the stone shrine, *nansipupinge,* in the center. In the *gwingwendi'e,* or standing formation, a line of women stands parallel to a line of men, with an evergreen tree at each end of the line. There is a total of about 40 dancers, singing a cappella, dancing in place using the antege step and from time to time pivoting and reversing the line orientation.

In the second or *mwe'ekwo* formation, the men are shoulder-to-shoulder, antegeing in place. The women kneel on a blanket, facing the men, and place their baskets upside down on the ground—the baskets are resonators for the *mwe'e* scraping sticks. The dance concludes with a short version of the standing dance. The dance is repeated three more times in the afternoon, using a different set of evergreen trees each time. Thus, the dance lines have faced each of the four cardinal directions at some time during the afternoon.

Easter dances in the pueblos are a preparation for the planting season—a prayer for the gift of life, plant and human, from generation to generation.

For more information on dances contact individual pueblo tribal offices. Photography is permitted with permission at San Juan for most of their dances and often at San Ildefonso. No photography is permitted at Jémez, or at any of the Keresan-speaking villages (Santo Domingo, San Felipe and Cochití). Only rarely are Easter dances given at Santa Clara Pueblo. The Catholic churches in the villages start Easter Sunday with Mass. The times for services vary from village to village, because many of the villages share the same Franciscan priest. Dancing begins about noon and continues to middle or late afternoon. Sometimes there is a break for lunch.

Pueblo Children

Text and photography by Stephen Trimble

Within a world bounded by sacred mountains, a Tewa Indian child is born. Four days later, as the sun rises from behind the Sangre de Cristo Mountains, the child is carried outside at dawn.

Two women present the small new person to the sun and to the six directions: north, west, south, east, zenith and nadir. They also offer two ears of perfect corn, one white and one blue. These "corn mothers" symbolize Blue Corn Woman and White Corn Maiden—the original mothers of the Pueblo people. The white light of the east burnishes the adobe walls of the Tewa Pueblos, of San Juan, Santa Clara and San Ildefonso; of Nambé, Pojoaque and Tesuque. The child receives its name.

During the first year of life, Tewa children go through the water-giving ceremony, first step on the path to becoming a member of one of the two religious divisions of the village.

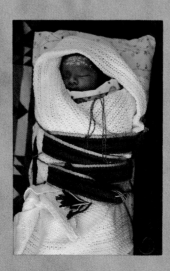

Sometime after the child is 6, the water-pouring ceremony ends childhood and finally, at 10 years of age, Tewa children become "finished" summer or winter people.

Long before this, they begin to dance. Everyone dances —and in doing so they ensure good things will come to all people. We participate in this renewal of life by watching, by listening, by being there. From the beginning the children dance and sing wholeheartedly, as one Tewa has said, "from the heart up."

Pueblo children grow up where their ancestors have lived for centuries. The continuity of their people and their place gives them an edge on strength, a foundation for growth, a potential certainty about who they are.

Imagine this life. Start with this base. Learn the traditions of your people. Live with your grandmother and great-grandmother. Become "finished" in ceremonial life, learn to pot, perhaps learn to weave. And learn to speak Tewa, for without the language, understanding the old way is impossible.

At the same time, you enter school and learn English; you begin the path toward the new way. And before you or

Along with their elders, Pueblo Indian children dance for the sacred renewal of life. The boy above is painted for a Comanche Dance at San Juan Pueblo. All of the other children are ready to participate in a Harvest Dance on Santa Clara Pueblo's feast day.

97

your parents know what has happened, in a few short years you have turned into a middle-class, All-American teenager as well as a Tewa Indian.

After high school, the pueblos offer few options for work. Go to college and risk losing the traditional values. Stay home and you must improvise a profession, supporting yourself by pottery, art or a salaried job in a nearby town. Difficult choices face you.

Indian people strive to keep their families together; four generations may live within a few steps of each other's doorways. But today brings change. Marrying outside the tribe means parents share only English as their common language, and children may not learn either parent's Indian language. Maintaining the old and excelling in the new means constant struggle. Somewhere within these conflicts there exists a balance.

My photographs show Pueblo children in ceremonial clothing, dressed for dances, for the sacred renewing of life. But there is no need to "dress like an Indian" to show you are traditional. A young Pueblo woman described it this way: "You may have on a pair of pants that say Calvin Klein, but that does not change the way you feel in your heart."

Dance is important in the life of a pueblo child. Costumes are sometimes imaginative, as illustrated by these young San Juan Comanche dancers. The San Ildefonso boy with the horn at top left is more traditionally attired; he is an animal dancer.

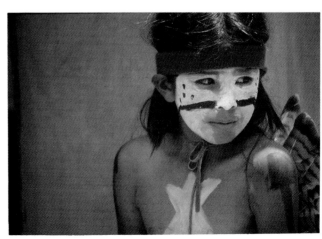

Focus on Indians
Howard T. Rainer documents the dignity of his people

As a young boy growing up in Taos Pueblo, Howard T. Rainer was genuinely fascinated by the cameras that tourists brought. While some elder Taos Indians had grown irritated by the clicking cameras, the young Indian boy was intrigued. He, too, however, noticed how intrusive some tourists were in their efforts to capture pueblo life. He'd witnessed tourists barging into homes and interrupting private services—even a family funeral.

Those experiences had a profound effect on him. "As a photographer, I do not intrude. I always ask for permission. It is a favor that someone gives when they allow you to photograph," Rainer says. For the past 15 years he has traveled across the country photographing American Indians. "Some Indian people have watched me intently before allowing their photographs to be taken. They want to be sure that I am who I say I am. When I put the camera down, they change into their smiles and we talk Indian to Indian."

Rainer now lives in Utah, where he is Project Administrator of Native American Educational Outreach Programs. His work as a national Indian consultant in motivation and positive self-discovery, self-image and youth leadership and development brings him to Indian people across the country. He always travels with his camera ready for that special shot.

A favorite stop is Taos Pueblo—his father, John C. Rainer of Taos Pueblo, and his mother, Wynema Rainer, a Creek Indian, still live nearby. "They've been real supporters and encouraged me in my work," he says.

He recalls when he was a boy in school and learning was a struggle. "I remember when I was going to the Taos Day School and there were only pictures of white people on the walls—George Washington, Dick and Jane. I remember thinking, 'Someday I'll do something about it.' . . . The fire was lit back then."

His early attempts were to become an artist. He struggled with painting and drawing. He wanted desperately to find a form of expression. But over and over he was told that he just didn't have the talent to be an artist.

He continued his education by studying at Bacone Junior College in Oklahoma and later earned both a bachelor's and master's degree in public relations and communication from Brigham Young University.

The real turning point in his life came in 1969. His grandmother was baking bread at Taos Pueblo that day and he asked if he could take her photograph. She replied in Tiwa, "Yes, I'll do it for you. Only you. But hurry before the others see."

"I was so pleased with the results," he says. "I realized that this was my vehicle for artistic expression." He gave the photograph to his grandmother and it has given him great pride to see that photograph hanging in her house.

by Emily Drabanski
Photography by Howard T. Rainer

Mike Reyna stands tall during the Taos Pueblo Powwow in July.

Sam Romero pauses at sundown during Taos Pueblo Powwow.

John Marcus waits to hear the drums during the San Gerónimo celebration at Taos Pueblo.

Opposite—Howard T. Rainer, who grew up in Taos Pueblo, took this photograph of John Marcus. Wrapped in a traditional Taos Pueblo winter blanket, Marcus heads to his winter home at sunset.

A buffalo skull and fluorescent purple chiles decorate the wall of the Moccasin Shop in Taos.

A Taos Pueblo couple sit in quiet summer solitude.

Snow gently falls around Marie Mondragon, creating a serene winter scene.

"For me, photography is more than a passion. It's therapeutic. It's everything. It just does something electric and I lose all sense of logic," he says, explaining his desire to get a photograph in spite of the odds.

He recalls a winter visit to Taos Pueblo when he conducted a self-image workshop at the same day school he attended as a child. The afternoon workshop was over and he realized that he was coming down with a serious flu. "I had the chills, a high fever, sore throat and ached painfully all over. I went to my parents' home for a brief moment and watched the snow gently fall against my parents' living room window. I was so discouraged because I wanted so badly to be outside and shooting because of the beautiful winter scene the snowfall was presenting."

He could no longer resist the temptation and headed for the pueblo. While driving, he saw an Indian woman that he had known as a boy. "I stopped the car and went over to see her. She was delighted to see me and as I conversed with her in Indian, I composed a photograph in my mind with the snow coming down and her wrapped in her beautiful red shawl. With Pueblo graciousness, she consented to have me pose her near an adobe wall and I pulled up my camera to shoot. My body shook and the aches cried out for attention, but for a few brief minutes I lost myself in total concentration."

He went home and collapsed. Was it worth the effort? "This picture I consider to be one of my finest and I shall never forget how I got it," he says.

"I am constantly trying to gather fragments of contemporary Indian life on film for future generations. There is something inside me wanting to visually document the good things our Indian people possess."

He notes that many photographers are interested in capturing the heartache, sorrow and turmoil found among the Indian people. "I could present this portion of reservation life, but I deemed it more important to afford my people and the non-Indian viewer with the representation of the abundance of goodness that prevails despite the hardships of life that hang at the doorsteps of every Indian community."

When asked why he photographs only in color, he responds, "Indian people love vivid, exciting colors, and I would lose half of their true image if I photographed them in black and white. Black and white has its own power and aura, but color best describes the truth. Indians aren't afraid to wear what pleases them."

He views his photography as a lifelong process. "I never stop striving to take that one shot that will stand alone with its own individual statement portraying Indian people with the dignity they rightfully deserve."

Left to right—Howard T. Rainer, John C. Rainer and Tony Reyna prepare for the San Gerónimo celebration. Howard T. Rainer's father, is a former spokesman for the pueblo. Reyna, Howard's uncle, is a former pueblo governor.

Coming of Age
Mescalero maidens graduate to womanhood

Joe Cavaretta

This detail shows the intricate artistry that goes into the dresses worn by girls in the Mescalero Apache Girls' Puberty Ceremonial. The girls are responsible for making their own dresses.

I n the blue light of pre-dawn, just before the sun tops East Mountain and the mesas to shine on the ceremonial arena, early risers sit on bleachers or stand stamping their feet against the chill. Everyone focuses on the center of the arena and on the men from whose fingers tiny streams of cattail pollen cascade in a blessing.

Wood smoke curls into the air, joined by smells of freshly cut oak boughs, pine and fir trees, chile stews and fry bread, promising a hearty breakfast. It is deep summer on the Mescalero Apache Reservation in south-central New Mexico and once again time for the celebration of womanhood, the Mescalero Apache Girls' Puberty Ceremonial.

Each year around July 4, Mescalero, Chiricahua and Lipan Apaches enrolled as members of the Mescalero Apache Tribe present their daughters publicly in one of the more colorful events on a contemporary Indian reservation. For four days and four nights, the girls' puberty ceremony continues with a series of events open to the public. Not only are the girls presented ritually and formally but related events are also scheduled: a rodeo with competition points available for the National Indian Rodeo Association Championship, a powwow featuring cash prizes for dancers, a parade on July 4 and the spectacular nighttime Dance of the Mountain Gods. Throughout, visitors are encouraged to eat Apache food prepared by the relatives of the girls in the ceremonial.

How did it begin? Why is it done today? Why is it always on the Fourth of July? What does it all mean?

According to the Apaches, when the world was being made, creation took four days. On the first day the celestial sphere and the earth were created along with sky elements (rain, lightning, clouds, thunder) and earth elements (rivers, dirt, rocks, plants).

Father Sky and Mother Earth were in their proper places among the newly created stars and planets. On the second day insects and flying things appeared. On the third day the animals of the world were made. On the fourth and final day, people, the Apaches, came into existence. They could not come into being until everything else was created, for

By Claire R. Farrer and Bernard Second
Photography by Joe Cavaretta and Claire R. Farrer

Joe Cavaretta

Melanie Kie, left, and Elaine Choneska celebrate their entry into womanhood during the puberty ceremonial.

Joe Cavaretta

Melanie Kie busily furrows one of the tepee poles that will be used in the ceremonial.

A Mescalero Apache singer, the late Bernard Second, paints a sun symbol on his hand in preparation for the last morning of the four-day coming-of-age ceremony.

people are the weakest ones in the association of beings, the ones who depend upon all the rest for their sustenance.

Soon White Painted Woman walked the Earth. She appeared in the east as a beautiful young woman. As she lived her life, she moved to the west where she disappeared, an old and revered lady. Miraculously, she reappeared in the east and again was young and beautiful.

Her name, Isdzanatl'eesh (*isdzan* = woman; *atl'eesh* = white painted), is the honorific name given each girl who has a puberty ceremonial at her own time of changing. On the last day of the four days of the public part of the ceremonial, a girl-woman's face and body are painted with white clay, as she enacts the role of White Painted Woman.

On both the first and last days of this part of the ceremonial, the girl must run around a basket four times to symbolize the four stages of life (infancy, childhood, adulthood, old age) set into motion by White Painted Woman. The runs also symbolize the journey White Painted Woman made on Earth from her home to the ends of the Earth and back again.

The basket around which the girls run represents industriousness, for it is a difficult task to find, gather and process the raw materials to make a basket. Inside the basket are items symbolizing each of the four days of creation.

During the ceremonial, a girl has a *naaikish*, or godmother, who shepherds her through the event, helping her to understand what she is to do and why she is to do it, massaging her legs when she tires from dancing and molding her body into that of a fine young woman. A girl also has a *gutaat*, a singer of ceremonies, who is always a man. Ideally, each girl has her own godmother and singer, but singers are in rather short supply and sometimes two girls will share a singer.

Each of the four nights of the ceremonial, the girls and godmothers, preceded by singers, enter the Holy Lodge, or Ceremonial Tepee, ritually erected on the morning of the first day. The girls dance each night inside the Holy Lodge, while the singers set the beat with their deer-hoof rattles and songs. These songs are not everyday tunes but holy in themselves; they are not to be recorded in any form; they are only to be committed to memory. The songs recapitulate the creation time as well as the history of the people from the beginning to the present. They are both bible and encyclopedia for the Mescalero Apache.

Boys and men wishing to become singers must have well-trained memories, for the songs and rituals they engender and accompany must proceed in a precise and unvarying order. Imagine trying to memorize several hours of text and

*Winifred Comanche, right, is pictured with her god-
mother-sponsor, Wilma Evans, after being bathed.
According to ceremonial tradition, the godmother
must bathe the girl on the morning of the last day
of the ceremonial.*

Medicine man Sidney Baca sprinkles corn pollen to bless a girl in the ceremonial.

melody for each of four nights of singing. It is a prodigious feat.

In the old days, before the coming of *indaa* (literally, enemy; colloquially, white people), the Mescalero people celebrated the physiological coming-of-age of their daughters. A small ceremony of a day or so would be performed immediately upon initial menses. The larger ceremony of four days and four nights would take place at a time when sufficient food and other resources could be mustered for the expected crowds of attending relatives and friends.

For the Mescalero, as for other Apaches and Navajos, one's primary kinship and descent are traced through the mother. Men and women are born into a matrilineage, a mother's line, in which they remain all their lives. Upon marriage, a proper Apache or Navajo man is expected to move into the area, if not the home, of his wife's parents. In matrilineages, strong bonds are created and maintained through life with one's sisters, brothers and first cousins through the mothers, as well as with the mother's sisters, brothers and so on through grandparental generations.

If your mother is an Apache, you are an Apache. Today, of course, Anglo law and custom are overlaid and one can be an enrolled member of the tribe through descent from an Apache father, too. Nonetheless, the primary kinship re-lationship remains the matrilineage. It is easy to understand why the puberty of a girl is celebrated. She will become "the mother of a tribe," as is often heard. Her children are what allows the tribe to continue in the future—as it has in the past.

Despite pressure to acculturate to the Anglo way of life, many young women on the reservation today choose a ceremonial, even though it places restrictions on them and makes requirements of them and their extended families. A tremendous expense is involved in hiring a singer, a godmother, a group of Mountain God dancers, in buying food and gifts, in preparing vast quantities of food for several days, in securing the elements of the ceremonial dress, including skins, beaded decorations and jewelry.

It is not necessary, however, to have a ceremonial to become a proper woman. And it is even possible to have a ceremony several years after menstruation, although such events are usually private.

The July date for the public celebration is a footnote to history. During the Indian Wars of the latter part of the 19th century, the Apaches were the last to capitulate to the United States government. Gerónimo's "capture" is the making of both history and folklore. Less known is that Mescaleros and other Apaches were imprisoned at Bosque

Most ceremonials are conducted in an isolated area of the reservation.

Redondo before the Navajos' Long Walk.

In 1873 the Mescalero Apache Reservation was established; those who were still at the Bosque, those who had walked away from there or other forts, as well as those from other prisoner sites, were placed on the reservation. They were not allowed to congregate, however. As the saying went, "More than six Apaches in one place constitutes an uprising."

It takes many more than six people to have a ceremonial. Some people say that ceremonials were held in secret, in the mountains far from the prying eyes of the military and the agents. Others say that no ceremonials were held, but the singers and godmothers kept the songs and actions in their hearts and minds until they could again be performed.

In 1911 the Army decreed that Indians on the Mescalero Apache Reservation could congregate on July 4 to celebrate the nation's birthday. By this time, those Indians were not just Mescaleros; they were also the remnants of the Lipan Apaches, Warm Springs Apaches, Tularosa Apaches and other small Apache groups. They were told that they could hold their ceremonial again but only on that date.

There was another consideration, too. Gerónimo's followers were still prisoners of war in Oklahoma, after having been imprisoned in Alabama and Florida. Negotiations were under way to move to Mescalero those who chose to be relocated. Many wanted to return to Arizona, but the choices were only Mescalero or Oklahoma. The Mescalero and Lipan Apaches decided to await the arrival of their cousins, the so-called Gerónimo Chiricahua Apaches, or the Fort Sills, before resuming the ceremonial. In 1913 the ceremonial was again staged publicly—on the Fourth of July.

Initially, the Apaches stayed with that date as a way of thumbing their noses at the United States government. What could be more insulting, even if subtle, than to hold the most Apachean celebration on the national holiday of the conquerers? What began as insult soon became tradition and convenience. Most Apaches are employed now and the Fourth of July is a holiday.

The meaning of the ceremonial is complex. Like any good celebration, it speaks to individuals on many levels. Some celebrate as homecoming, seeing friends and relatives, and renewing ties. Others celebrate in a religious fashion, fully believing that as long as the religion is intact, the Apaches will survive. For some it is a time of license, while for many it is a time to rejoice in being Indian, specifically Apache, and to show Anglos what hospitality and generosity really mean. For those whose daughters are par-

Joe Cavaretta

Nighttime dancing of the Mountain Gods is an important part of the puberty rites ceremonial.

ticipating, it is a time both of immense pride and enormous work requiring many hours.

Oftentimes local newspapers refer to the ceremonial as if it were a debutante ball. But families do not have to be wealthy—other than in relatives—to have their daughters presented in the event. The tribe, through its council, funds a portion of the expenses for those who choose the July date for their daughters.

As an example, the parents of two daughters under 7 are already planning for the ceremonials. They will spend a minimum of $3,500 out-of-pocket for each girl. This money is for presents and cash to the singer, godmother, the owner of the inherited rights to the songs to be used and the designs to be painted on the group of Mountain God dancers, for cloth and tobacco presents to those who dance all night on the fourth night, for skins to make the exquisite ceremonial dress and moccasins, for beads to decorate clothing and for food purchases. The mother is already planning a collection of large pots and pans that she will need in a few years.

By helping now with the ceremonials of their own relatives' daughters, the parents ensure that they will have help in the future. What goes around comes around, as the saying goes. But debutante is a misnomer for a girl having her

ceremonial unless one thinks of the term meaning a young woman rich in relatives willing to help.

But no debutante's family is more proud of her than are Apache parents. As a mother said recently when looking at a photograph of her own daughter's ceremonial in 1984, "It just makes me so proud when I see her dressed like that. She is a good girl. Her family is proud of her."

The hard work fades from memory. The cooking for hundreds, three meals a day each day, is remembered as a routine accompanied by women's laughter—women in one's family, perhaps the women married to brothers and uncles and those good friends who willingly peel potatoes, shape fry bread, roast chiles and stir stews. The hours spent lugging 25-pound sacks of flour, slaughtering beef, working skins, beading, sewing tepee covers, getting sore fingers and hands from punching an awl through tough hide for moccasin soles—all blur in the glow of pride from successfully launching a daughter into womanhood.

The Mescalero Apache Tribe welcomes visitors to the reservation for the annual July ceremonial. Write the tribe at P.O. Box 176, Mescalero, N.M. 88340 for details. Remember you are watching a religious event, with entertainment interspersed. Cameras and tape recorders are prohibited, as is note taking. 🔥

Above—The 17th-century mission church of San Estevan Rey dominates the Sky City from the west, with a centuries-old natural water cistern in the foreground. *Right*—Mount Taylor in the distance, as seen from the rock of Ácoma.

Mark Nohl

Ácoma
Sky City: Venerable and venerated, faces the future

A jagged old molar sticking up from the toothless plain—this is the great Rock of Acuco, the peñol of Ácoma, 60 miles west of Albuquerque and 14 miles south of Interstate 40. And perched on its flat top, 357 feet high, about the height of a 40-story skyscraper, the pueblo colorfully called the Sky City.

Capt. Hernando de Alvarado of Coronado's expedition of 1540, the first European of record to see it, reported that he "found a rock with a village on top, the strongest position ever seen in the world," naming it Acuco. It is generally assumed that Ácoma derives its name from Akóme, "people of the white rock" as the people call themselves, although the root *Ako* has no known etymology.

It was long ago, according to their migration myth, when the people were wandering the earth to find a home. The spirits, the kachinas, *told them the place would be called Ako. Masewi and Oyoyewi, the sacred twins, were leading the people. So every so often Masewi would stop and call out, "A-a-a-ko-o-o!" There was no answer, and the people wandered on. One day they stopped in front of a huge white rock. "Aaaakoooo-o-o!" Masewi called out in a loud voice, and the rock echoed it back clear and strong. "This is Ako!" he announced. So the people settled at the foot of the east point of the mesa, still called Ako-haiítitu. Then after a council they moved up on top.*

Tradition persists that some of the people first lived on top of Katzimo, the Enchanted Mesa, another nearby and precipitous butte 73 feet higher. When a storm blocked the path to it by a landslide, they moved to this forbidding cliff rock with the others.

This Keres pueblo of Ácoma in New Mexico contends with the Hopi pueblo of Oraibi in Arizona for the distinction of being the oldest continuously occupied settlement in the United States. Oraibi today is virtually an archaeological ruin of falling walls in which live scarcely a dozen families. Ácoma, in contrast, is a well-kept village regarded as home by 4,350 people who live on the reservation, one of the largest of New Mexico's 19 Indian pueblos. Throughout its long and tempestuous history, it has had the will to live and it still has.

How ancient the pueblo is no one knows. Certainly it long antedates the first settlement of English Pilgrims in 1620 marked by an inconspicuous boulder on the Atlantic shore of Plymouth harbor. Sherds found at Ácoma indicate the site has been occupied for at least a thousand years.

In prehistoric times the people lived as a self-contained unit on their lofty mesa between the immeasurable expanse of sky and the vast empty plain seamed with low outcrops of rock and long *cañadas* dark with juniper. So it is easy for us today to speak of the people as a collective unity enduring as an unbroken continuity through the centuries. The old died, the new were born. But the communal pattern remained the same. In little *milpas* below their home rock they cultivated corn, squash, beans and cotton and raised flocks of turkeys. The crops were dependent upon rain, and during droughts the people suffered. Gradually they ventured six leagues north to a place now called Cubero. It lay in a *cañada* perhaps a league long and half a league wide, watered by a little stream. Here they could irrigate their crops.

by Frank Waters

Richard C. Sandoval

Homes are being restored on a site that has been occupied for more than a thousand years.

Occasionally enemies came: "Apaches so insolent," reported a later Spanish priest, "that if this pueblo were not by nature defensible, perhaps nothing now would remain of it." The Ácomas then fled to the summit of their mesa, climbing tortuous trails formed by ladders and toe- and finger-holes cut into the rock and hurling down boulders and rocks upon their pursuers.

On top they were prepared to withstand a long siege. The bare flat sandstone comprised barely 70 acres. It was split in half by a deep narrow cleft. To the north stood three parallel blocks of communal buildings of two or three stories each, built of stones and adobe. Since there was no soil on the rocky surface, all the earth used to make adobe had to be carried in buffalo-hide bags up from the plain.

The only water on top was preserved in natural cisterns in the bedrock. Fray Francisco Atanasio Domínguez in 1776 described the largest on the south half of the mesa as "a cistern which God made in the rock itself. Its opening must be about 40 *varas* in circumference, and it must be fully as deep. Rain water is caught in it, and when it snows the Indians take care to collect all the snow they can. . . . In order that the rain water may be clean when it goes in, they are careful to keep the space around it swept, and there is a guard to prevent pollution. The water collected in this usually half fills it. Because the rock is solid, it has never been known to become fetid, and is always fresh although turbid."

How quiet and peaceful it is up here on a frosty Sunday morning in February. A few children are playing in a street. At the edge of the mesa a middle-aged man with a weather-beaten face is chopping wood. He is one of the perhaps 80 people who live here year-round, grazing his cattle below. "Good air, good water. No trouble from anybody."

Most of the Ácomas live down in Anzac or McCartys, and at Acomita, near the Santa Fe railroad line and the highway 15 miles north. Here they can put their children in school. But in the summer some 250 of them return to their homes in Ácoma. Others work in nearby towns. Mrs. Pablita Concho lives in McCartys, but she comes to Ácoma to open her small Sky City Curio Shop. Groceries, pottery, corn necklaces she obtains by trade from Cochití, odds and ends. So here she sits alone beside a tiny woodstove, perfectly content. Sturdy Mr. Pino in 1940, at the age of 33, was the youngest man ever to be elected governor of Ácoma. For 28 years he worked for the Santa Fe as a "track man." Now he lives in Anzac, but still regards Ácoma as home.

How quiet it is up here and so peaceful. But up above sounds the drone of a transcontinental airliner. And then comes a sonic boom. Built on the bedrock, the buildings have no foundations; the walls shake. The ominous sound of change.

The first change came with the Spaniards. Coronado's

discovery expedition of 1540 was followed by the *entrada* of Antonio de Espejo and other small parties. Not until 1598 did Juan de Oñate make the first successful effort to colonize the country. His impressive train comprised 400 men and their families, 83 baggage carts and 7,000 head of stock. Receiving the *obediencias* of many pueblos on the Río Grande, he dispatched Don Juan de Zaldívar with 31 men to Ácoma in the "Kingdom of Acus." It was then Ácoma gained the reputation of being the most treacherous and intractible of all pueblos.

On Dec. 1, 1598, Zaldívar reached the great fortress and camped two leagues away. Three days later, with 18 men, he ascended the rock to get some cornmeal the Indians had promised him. Without warning, the chief, Zutucapan, and his warriors attacked the Spanish detachment. Zaldívar and 12 of his men were killed, the survivors escaping back to Oñate.

Oñate then dispatched another force of 70 men under Juan de Zaldívar's brother, Vicente, to avenge his brother's death and punish Ácoma. Included in the detachment was the soldier-poet Gaspar Perez de Villagrá.

Their assault of the Sky City began on Jan. 22, 1599, and lasted for three days. While most of the soldiers engaged the Indians at the ladder trails, Villagrá with 12 men gained the summit of the south section separated from the village area by the deep cleft in the rock. With a celebrated leap, Villagrá cleared the chasm and threw logs across to bridge it. Then he and his companions joined the main force hacking its way into the pueblo.

The Spaniards burned the town, killing more than 600 Ácomas and taking nearly 600 prisoners. Some 70 captured warriors were confined in a kiva. From here they were taken out one by one, murdered and thrown over the cliff. The remaining 500 captives, most of them women and children, Zaldívar marched to Santo Domingo to stand trial. Here in February, Oñate, finding them guilty of killing 11 Spaniards and their two servants, pronounced sentence. All males of more than 25 years of age were condemned to have one foot cut off and to give 20 years of personal service to the Spaniards; the males between 12 and 25 years, and all females, were doomed to servitude.

This conquest of Ácoma was celebrated by Villagrá's epic poem *The History of New Mexico,* published in Spain in 1610. Villagrá himself transported 60 or 70 of the young captive girls to the viceroy in Mexico. It is an interesting corollary that his daughter married the grandnephew of Moctezuma, the last Aztec emperor of Mexico, conquered by Cortés, and that Oñate himself married the great-granddaughter of Moctezuma. These two men thus helped to father the nucleus of a new mixed race of Spanish-Indian blood on the American continent, the mestizo.

Oñate's colonization of New Mexico seemed well established under harsh Spanish rule. Every pueblo household was required to pay in tribute one *vara* (33 inches) of cotton cloth. Indians were flogged for infringement of the laws. People were enslaved to labor for the crown and the Church, and their native worship was regarded as idolatry.

Ácoma stubbornly survived under this regime. Then in 1629 Fray Juan Ramírez was escorted to the pueblo by the governor of New Mexico, Francisco Manual Silva Nieto, as its first permanent missionary. Father Ramírez was a stout Franciscan. Envisioning a church on the citadel, he built a trail to the top named after him—*El Camino del Padre,* the Path of the Father. He then directed the building of the so-called Burro Trail, which could be used for packing up materials for the erection of the church.

There is some controversy today as to just when the church was built. Consensus is that it was constructed by Ramírez between 1629 and 1641. The church was dedicated to the first martyr, San Estevan (St. Stephen), the original patron saint of Ácoma. But as his feast day came on Dec. 26, coinciding with Christmas, the celebration was later changed to the feast day of St. Stephen, the King of Hungary, on Sept. 2, the church taking the name of San Estevan Rey.

Construction was extremely difficult. Embracing an area 150 feet long and 40 feet wide, the walls were 60 feet high and 10 feet thick. The great logs for the roof *vigas,* 40 feet long and 14 inches square, were cut in the Cebolleta Mountains 30 miles away. Building the adjoining cemetery was another feat. A rock retaining wall 40 feet high was constructed on the edge of the mesa, and the 200-foot square was filled with earth, all this material being hauled up from the valley below.

During the last three centuries the church has suffered minor damage and parts of it have been rebuilt. The outer walls were resurfaced in 1970 with a layer of cut-stone, all the labor done by Ácoma workmen without pay; men unable to contribute work were required to pay a dollar a day. Every year it is replastered on the outside. However, as authorities assert: "The great church at Ácoma probably incorporates more of the original structure than any of the

Richard C. Sandoval

Water from rain and snow is collected in rock cisterns in Ácoma.

surviving 17th-century churches in New Mexico. . . . In this sense it has strong claim to consideration as the 'oldest church.'" Certainly San Estevan Rey is one of the most beautiful and imposing mission churches in the Southwest, if not in the United States: an enduring monument to both Spanish and Ácoma faith.

Meanwhile, during its construction, Indian rebellion against the Spanish crown was being slowly organized by Popé, a medicine man working from Taos Pueblo. On Aug. 10, 1680, every pueblo rebelled, the Ácomas murdering Fray Lucas Maldonado Olasqueaín, the current priest. In all, the Indians killed nearly 500 Spaniards, including 21 friars at their altars, tore down churches, destroyed government and church records, "vented their fury on the hens, the sheep, the fruit trees of Castille, and even upon the wheat" and washed the heads of all baptized Indians to cleanse them of the Spanish stain. The surviving Spaniards fled back to Mexico.

Again in 1692 a new wave of conquest rolled in with Don Diego de Vargas, Zapata y Luján, Ponce de León on its crest. This time de Vargas with much diplomacy promised forgiveness to all pueblos that would submit to Spanish rule. He then marched westward with his small army. In November 1693 he reached a spring, El Pozo, from which he could see the *peñol* of Ácoma. As he wrote in his journal: "We described the smoke made by those traitors, enemies, treacherous rebels, and apostates of the Zueres [Keres] tribe." Finally, with much persuasion, he induced them to parley. But not until 1699 did Ácoma formally submit to Spanish rule.

The advantages soon became apparent to the Ácomas. The Spaniards were introducing horses, cattle and sheep, fruit trees, new customs and a new faith. So after nearly two centuries there began that amalgamation of Spanish and Indian cultures that characterizes New Mexico today.

The Ácomas today are almost wholly devout Catholics. Almost every Ácoma bears a Spanish name. But none of them speak Spanish, as do the pueblos along the Río Grande.

The coming of the "Americans" brought another, shorter period of change. Following Gen. Stephen Kearny's bloodless march of conquest from the Missouri to Santa Fe and the war between Mexico and the United States, all of New Mexico was ceded by Mexico to the United States by the Treaty of Guadalupe Hidalgo in 1848.

Spain in 1551, under King Charles V, had provided land grants to each pueblo with water rights, farming lands and mountains. This law was confirmed by the Royal Council of the Indies on June 4, 1687. Mexico, after winning independence from Spain, had in turn confirmed the pueblos' titles to their communally owned land grants. And now the United States in 1858 was the third nation to confirm the Ácoma title to its land.

Five years later Ácoma sent its governor with those of six other pueblos to visit President Abraham Lincoln in Washington. Settling boundaries to their grants, President Lincoln presented the governors with silver-headed canes as a token of their right to govern their own affairs. On the cane presented to the governor of Ácoma was engraved:

A. Lincoln
Prst. U.S.A.
Acoma
1863

This cane was passed to each succeeding governor when he was elected in January, constituting his badge of office. The governor today still carries the cane to all official functions.

Soon after the Americans came, nearby Laguna Pueblo, founded after the Spanish conquest, began to suffer from droughts and epidemics. In an effort to stop these calamities, Laguna requested from Ácoma the loan of the painting of St. Joseph. The painting, said to have been presented to the church in 1690 by King Charles II of Spain, was believed to possess miraculous powers. Ácoma consented to the loan. When it was taken to Laguna, the pueblo's misfortunes ceased, but Laguna refused to return it. Lots were drawn to decide its ownership. Ácoma won and the painting was escorted back home.

Then at Mass one morning, the Ácomas noticed that their sacred painting was gone. War with Laguna was averted only by Father Lopez's advice to take the matter to the United States court in Santa Fe. The decision was in Ácoma's favor, but Laguna appealed the case to the Supreme Court. The final ruling in 1857 was again in Ácoma's favor. Rejoicing, a committee started to Laguna to bring back the painting. Halfway there, they found it under a tree. St. Joseph, hearing of the decision, had started to return home; but being wearied, he had tarried under a tree to rest.

A less charming story, but a more significant event, happened in 1933. Acoma had a population of some 1,000 people. The land could not support them. As irrigated farming could not be extended, they had come to depend upon the raising of sheep and cattle. But the eroded range could support only 8,500 of the 33,000 sheep "units" being grazed upon it. If its land was to survive, Ácoma would have to reduce its flocks.

John Collier, the U.S. commissioner of Indian affairs who had introduced into Congress the Indian Reorganization Act, went to Ácoma and laid the facts before the 70-year-old governor and his council. The stock reduction was not a command from the national government; other tribes had rejected it.

As Collier wrote later: "The whole deep, living past of

Tradition says the people first lived atop nearby Enchanted Mesa.

Mark Nohl

Ácoma, with the vision of ages to come and of the land to be saved for those ages, slowly absorbed the new facts and adopted their challenge. The thing was done. Ácoma effected the crushing reduction. . . . It was within their society, for their society, by virtue of its powers, that the people of Ácoma flashed beyond the world-present into the world-future."

It was another manifestation of Ácoma's obdurate will to live and to preserve its homeland despite all changes. Stock control is still enforced, the number of head of stock varying year by year according to the rainfall. Water is still a great problem, as it was in prehistoric times. Ácoma has no rich natural resources to develop; it still depends on its land for stock grazing and marginal farming.

But its population is increasing. Besides the great mission, there are three other mission churches on the reservation. And new schools are preparing children for the world-future.

Some 305 Ácoma children from kindergarten through eighth grade attend Sky City Community School in Acomita, and the modern Laguna-Ácoma High School serves older students. Some attend schools in Grants; school buses carry them back and forth from Acomita and McCartys. All are growing up in the modern world, proud of being Ácomas.

Change, change, change, a perpetual tide of change beating against the great rocks of Acuco, the *peñol* of Ácoma. Railroad, highway, airliners, sonic booms and tourists. You can drive up on the top of the mesa now, after a stop at the Tourist Center below. There a pleasant, courteous Ácoma collects the admission fees. The pueblo is open seven days a week.

In past years Ácoma's native ceremonialism was rich and profound, with its many rituals, kachinas, pahos, koshares and masked dances. Today there are few evidences of the forms of this ancient faith. There are no great ceremonies such as those held in the Hopi pueblos, Zuñi, Santo Domingo and others. One wonders, completely

Richard C. Sandoval

Earth to build adobes had to be carried up from the plain.

Roman Catholic as the people are, if their ancient faith in the verities of earth and sky is forgotten.

"We don't talk about these things," an old man told me. "They are sacred and secret, but they are still observed. We are Indians yet!"

But there are held a number of colorful public functions combining Indian, Spanish and American influences. On Aug. 10, San Lorenzo Day, and on July 26, Santa Ana Day, Corn Dances are given. On June 24, San Juan Day, on June 29, San Pedro Day, and on July 25, San Diego Day, come the rooster pulls. Atop the mesa in the morning, men and boys run underneath a rooster hanging above them—they run under it many times, as a form of prayer. At a certain time the rooster is taken down and raced around the village. In late afternoon, at the bottom of the mesa, the ceremony is repeated, this time with men and boys on horseback. When the racing is finished, the people return to the top of the mesa for a food throw. All households whose occupants bear the names of Peter, James or John throw down food from their rooftops on their particular saint's day to the crowd below, commemorating the time when persons bearing these names were responsible for providing food to the village. In February, on Governor's Day, Eagle, Deer and Comanche dances are given.

The most important function is the great procession on Sept. 2, the Day of San Estevan, Ácoma's patron saint. Indian, Spanish and Anglo-Americans come from miles around. After Mass in the great church, the saint is carried throughout the pueblo and set in a little shelter of green boughs. All afternoon groups of dancers perform before him. Then he is carried back into the church. In the evening "fiesta" lasts until late with traditional social dancing.

Weaving and other handicrafts have been given up. But the famous Ácoma pottery, the thinnest of all pueblo pottery, is still being made: the exquisite shapes, the delicate color from vegetable pigments, the decorative styling of birds and flowers.

In the good old days the women of Ácoma would squat beside the dirt road curving below McCartys, their wares spread out on the blankets for a half-mile. Times have changed. Nowadays on a straight speedway, I-40, the cars hurtle past too fast to stop. Where are they all going in such a hurry? No matter. The women still make pots.

Lucy Lewis was a famous potter of my earlier days. Her ceramic owls grace my shelves and those of many museums. She is getting a little too old to make them now. From her mother she learned the art, and her mother from her mother before that; she has taught her children and neighbors. Brown hands still shaping the shapes of centuries, unchanged despite the changes.

There is something about Ácoma pottery that reveals the enduring essence of Ácoma character beneath its changing personality. It is possible that the same invisible forces of earth and sky are also shaping its human lives through their period of greatest change. Could it be possible that, in this tragic era when we are making an ecological fight for survival, this one of the first communities in America may also be one of the last?

The Dinetah-Navajo Sacred Homeland

Holy place reveals Navajo origins, provides strength

Medicine men from across the Navajo Nation study the petroglyphs in the Dinetah area. This petroglyph tells the story of Monster Slayer.

When Irene Tsinijinnie was a young girl, there were no televisions. In fact, on the Navajo Reservation it was hard to find even a radio. Growing up in Round Rock, Ariz., she spent her spare time listening to stories of a time long ago.

"I remember," she recalls, "sitting in the hogan listening to my father, Ashihie, who was a medicine man, tell stories of a sacred place called Dinetah. This place, my father would say, is where medicine men are supposed to go and check to see the proper way to make the masks and other ceremonial items the Holy People taught the Navajos to use."

Dinetah is a Navajo word meaning "homeland." Accord-

Story and photography by Monty Roessel

Two buttes named after the Twins—Child Born for Water at left, Monster Slayer at right—stand guard at the entrance to the Dinetah.

ing to Navajo beliefs, when Changing Woman went to the Western Ocean to live with her husband, the Sun, she left Navajo people living in the Dinetah area. She created more Navajos by rubbing parts of her body, and these new Navajos wanted to return to their original homeland—Dinetah. When they did, they found the Navajos who were already living there.

It is difficult to convey the place Dinetah occupies in the history of the Navajos. Today, many Navajos don't even know where or what it is. Others have heard stories about the place but know nothing else. Yet to Navajo medicine men, it is a sacred and holy place where many Navajo stories have their origins.

Dinetah lies largely in the northwestern part of New Mexico about 40 miles southeast of Bloomfield. Oil and gas wells dot the landscape, with the sounds of pumping wells echoing through the canyon walls. It is a rugged beauty.

The bittersweet smell of sagebrush helps one look past the churning wells and explore a culture that existed here hundreds of years ago.

In the 1950s, appearing before the Indian Claims Court, the Navajos offered evidence of early Navajo occupation ranging from Chimney Rock in southwestern Colorado to the Abiquiú area in the Chama Valley in north-central New Mexico to Quemado, south of Zuñi. Dinetah comprises the center of this area, encompassing the Largo, Carizzo and Blanco canyon regions southeast of Farmington.

The Navajo land claims case was authorized by a 1947 act of Congress that authorized Indian tribes to sue the U.S. Government for improper and incorrect payment of land taken by the United States or early settlers. The claims case located five early Navajo sites dating in the 1300s. This is far earlier than many archaeologists believe the Navajos were in the area. Navajo stories support the earlier dates.

Another view of the petroglyph depicting Monster Slayer. The circle at far right has a bow in the center that is a representative symbol of Monster Slayer. The inner circle of the center circular figure represents the earth. Radiating from the earth are drawings of lightning that touch the outer circle, which is surrounded by cloud symbols.

Petroglyphs (rock carvings) and pictographs (rock paintings) made by Navajos in the 1600s and 1700s fill the canyon walls in Dinetah. These rock drawings contain Navajo Holy People and tell of their exploits and deeds.

One wall tells the story of the Gambler, who in Navajo mythology wins various games of chance. Aided by other Holy People, the Gambler participated in games of chance, primarily with the far richer Pueblos. He won every game, gaining large amounts of turquoise, shell and other jewelry. One of the pictographs displays the Gambler with a hoop and another shows a game of stick dice.

Many of the figures carved and painted on the canyon walls are identical to figures used in contemporary Navajo sand paintings. This surely attests to the relative absence of change for these aspects of Navajo religion.

Dinetah remains the Navajos' holy land. It is the source of strength and power for medicine men—a place to cleanse their thoughts and create, once again, harmony within their lives.

Billy Sam, a Navajo medicine man from Many Farms, Arizona, tells of the significance of Dinetah. "Many of our early stories took place in Dinetah. It was here that First Man saw the cloud set on Gobernador Peak. After four days First Man and First Woman went on top and found Changing Woman, who was a small baby. Years were only days and in 12 days they held Kinaalda' [the puberty ceremony for girls].

"It is here the Sun slept with Changing Woman and gave her twin boys, Monster Slayer and Child Born for Water. The boys, however, did not know who their father was. After meeting Spider Woman, they received prayers that enabled them to safely visit their father, the Sun. After visiting their father on the western ocean, they were allowed to return to their home, Huérfano Mesa."

Huérfano Mesa (Dzilna'ooldlii), about 20 miles south of Bloomfield on N.M. 44, is the site of the home of First Man and First Woman and where they raised Changing Woman.

The Navajos built their homes in fortified locations and lived peacefully with the Pueblos, who moved to Navajo land during the late 1600s to escape the Spaniards. At some Dinetah sites, Navajos in forked-stick hogans lived side by side with Pueblos residing in *pueblitos*.

Aside from the rock art, the most noticeable attractions are the forts that literally dot the landscape, much like the oil wells do now. Each fort is strategically placed to overlook a section of the land. Here the Navajos were able to scout for Utes, Comanches and Spaniards.

The most striking of these forts is Shaft Ruin. It is built into an upper wall of Crow Canyon, a side canyon off Largo Canyon. About one-half mile to the west is a small outpost that was used to scout the enemy. Shaft Ruin has portholes, about 5 inches in diameter, from which the Navajos shot arrows. Each hole is strategically angled so all possible approaches to Shaft Ruin are covered.

Pothunters and vandals threaten the area. This photo shows where a jackhammer was used in an attempt to remove a pictograph from a canyon wall.

Pressure from the Spaniards, Utes and Comanches finally forced the Navajos to move out of their beloved homeland. By the 1760s all Navajos had left the area. But they left their rock drawings, their homes and many of their sacred objects behind.

Because of roads connecting the oil wells in this sacred land, the rock art and ruins are easy to reach. This easy access, however, has its drawbacks. Dinetah has attracted pothunters and other people who not only desecrate the drawings and sites but also destroy and remove artifacts. Holes are drilled in the canyon walls, and panels that contain drawings of sacred figures are removed. Small caves in the area once contained sacred wooden objects made by the Navajos and Pueblos hundreds of years ago. Many of these artifacts now rest in museums or in someone's living room.

The Dinetah is principally managed by the U.S. Bureau of Land Management. The BLM rangers have law enforcement authority to prosecute individuals who are either removing or destroying artifacts, but because of the remoteness of the area, it is difficult to keep pothunters out.

Though more than 90 percent of Dinetah is federal land, there are small pieces of private property. Little is Navajo owned and most lies outside the Navajo Reservation. The tribe, however, is negotiating to lease and purchase land that is privately owned in an effort to reclaim part of its sacred homeland.

To the south, near Blanco, there are two buttes named after the Twins, Monster Slayer and Child Born for Water, that stand guard over the entrance to the Dinetah. As Tsinijinnie says, "Dinetah is very sacred to us; it is our Holy Land. We must protect it so our young people will know their homeland. Right now, the Twins are the only ones protecting our homeland."

Native American Portfolio

Eduardo Fuss

William Clark

Above—*Olla maidens.* **Above, right**—*Monica Jojola of Isleta Pueblo, the 1988-89 Miss Indian New Mexico.* **Bottom**—*Terry Sandoval, left, a Navajo from Torreon, and Pete Oka, a Blackfoot of the Blood Reservation in Alberta, Canada dress in traditional costumes.* **Right**—*Chester Mahooty, a member of the Rainbow Dance Troupe, proudly wears the costume and jewelry distinctive to his native Zuñi Pueblo.* **Following page**—*A fancy dancer's costume glistens in the movement of the night under the light of the Indian Village at the New Mexico State Fair.*

William Clark

127